Little Girls Secrets and Their Heroes

BASED ON A TRUE STORY OF SEXUAL ABUSE

JUDAH CLARKE

CONTENTS

Introduction	vii
Prologue	1
1. What Is Love?	3
2. Showing The Bruise	16
3. The Punishment System	39
4. The Aftermath	58
5. The Therapy	68
6. The Reliving	88
7. The Family Way	94
8. The Hope	104
9. The Set Up	112
10. The Rescue	124
11. Getting On With The Now	130
12. The Temporary Reprieve For Mara	140
13. The Martyr	146
14. The Convincing and The Relocation	154
15. The Insanity	162
16. The Angel	170
17. The Beginning of the Healing	191
18. The Con, The System and the Repeated Victimization	199
Epilogue	209
About the Author	211

©2022 Judah Clarke. All Rights Reserved.

Dedicated to sexual abuse survivors

INTRODUCTION

Little girls have carried quite a load in many cultures for many years. In the last sixty years an epidemic of hardship has come to them in the Southern United States. How ironically that one research has proven Alabama to hold the unfortunate record of having the highest incest rate in the nation over the past twenty years. Alabama just happens to be located in the Bible Belt and where Rachel Thane grew to womanhood. Her troubled past included a mother who was institutionalized when she was four; an older brother who, largely in charge, molested her from that time until he went to Vietnam in 1967 and she was left with almost no supervision. In her frightening memories which materialized through nightmares she reached out to her only stability at age 9, her Daddy. But her daddy molested her, misunderstanding her need. In her desperate search for security, all that was left for her was to take what little knowledge she could glean about God and go forward. This is based on the true story about a time which would have been a challenge for anyone, but for someone like Rachel, it is a miracle she continues to thrive.

Little Girls Secrets and Their Heroes is based on a true story of the sexual abuse of two little girls struggles for life in the aftermath of rape at the age of six years old, repeated over a 21-month period. Her younger sister whom she tried to protect was just out of diapers around two years of age and was sodomized for at least a six-month period, if not longer. This is based on their real-life drama as told to me by Rachel's mother.

PROLOGUE

The number one need of a child who has been sexually abused is security and stable acceptance. As we are created sexual beings, without the protection of a psychologically well parent from sexual abuse or neglect, the recovery of a sexual abuse victim is very minimal. The entire core of their existence has been shaken and, in some cases, crushed. The stability that other children experience is a dream for them, an idealistic, ethereal hope that they yearn to achieve, never seeming to measure up.

In the hope of understanding this deficiency, related here is a factual group of events *(names changed to protect the vulnerable)*, revealing the struggles, courage and freedom of at least one victim through the power of Light and Love, Father Time and the Hope of Glory to erase the Dark Ages of shame.

CHAPTER 1
WHAT IS LOVE?

Lying still as death on a too soft mattress, Mara Lenore DeVaughn drifted in Morpheus. Clouds of sunshine limned pillows floated aimlessly around her head in space, as her cherubic body glided in and out of a reddish black room flashing lights. Her soft rounded cheeks drew up as she squinted to see what was lurking in the corridor between the lights and the surrealism, she so desired to remain in. She knew something was there. She didn't know how she knew. She just knew. With each flash she saw doors that seemed to be one on top of another, slightly staggered like dominos and she couldn't tell if they were opened or closed. She wanted out. She turned to see if the pillow clouds were still there, knowing they weren't and felt the hair on the back of her neck porcupine up. As she slowly turned back, she saw in her peripheral vision, a beast. Black in color and etched with red. He resembled a man-sized monkey with a dragon tail and his talons were poised to pounce. She screamed and quickly turned to run but her feet,! Oh, they were stuck in ankle deep goo, and she could barely lift them! She knew the dragon would overtake her! He always did...

Mara snapped up in her bed with a gasp, clawing the air and trying to catch her breath. Sweat covered the outline of her soft caramel colored hair leaving it stuck to her face and neck and making her look as if she'd been in a sauna. The cool cotton nightgown clung to her chubby child's body like a second skin and as she focused on the familiar surroundings of her room, her heart slugged methodically against her prepubescent chest so loud she could almost hear it. She glanced down at the floor where her worn teddy bear lay in a heap looking as if she'd only just pushed him off her cozy bed. Her slippers were placed neatly beside her bureau and the soft light above the stove in the kitchen glided in through the crack in her door giving the room a shadowy look. Mara laid back on her pillow with a sigh of relief upon realizing she was in her own room. *Safe. Mama's house. Safe*, and she prayed, "God, please, please, don't let the dragon get me, again. Please, God".

Tears wet her pillow as her exhausted body slipped back asleep.

Two doors down the hall, Mara's mother rested fitfully as she went over the day's events. Fear seized her gut as she recalled the standoff with Mara's dad when he'd brought Mara and her little sister, Jenny home after the regular weekend visit at his house a mere two and a half miles away. He'd been drinking, again. Only this time she'd seen the evidence and knew it was her one and only opportunity to lawfully keep the children from his careless grasp. The past two and a half years had been a nightmare of accidents and inappropriate behavior and it was high time she did something about it. This was her ticket and by George she was using it. No more Miss Nice Girl...

The problem was, Henry DeVaughn didn't usually play by the rules, and she had no idea what he would do once he realized he couldn't get the children anymore, at all. She'd gathered every bit of mature grit three and a half years prior just to get the nerve to leave him knowing when she was pregnant with Jenny that the relationship was doomed for disaster with no chance at all for amiable coexistence. Henry's 6'6", 250 lb. frame, coupled with his appetite for drugs and alcohol had reached a level of danger that had put the entire family at risk. Rachel's house had been broken into, money and a television had been stolen. Henry had been offered $1000.00 a week, a new model Trans Am, and a sawed-off shotgun to run cocaine and crystal meth from central Alabama to northwest Florida the week before she'd finally gotten up the nerve to leave.

Rachel had pleaded with him for two years to turn his back on the irresponsible, destructive lifestyle they had been living and come with her to church, to God, to counseling, to whatever it took to get better but he was uninterested in changing his way of life, he had it just like he liked it and had simply pacified Rachel enough to make her stay. He would even threaten horrible consequences should she ever try to leave him, promising that no one would ever look at her again when he finished with her if he ever caught her trying to leave. The terrorist/victim relationship had worked for close to 10 years of Rachel's already traumatic life but no more. The terror stopped here. She wouldn't let her children go through the hell she'd been forced to endure.

Rachel had bided her time until she'd been able to devise a plan of escape that would see her and the girls safely from his terrifying grasp. It had taken a year and a half. Rachel had stayed in church and gotten a few good friends. When the opportunity arose, she had gone to work with the State of Alabama as a temporary clerical aide with the help of Felicia Kahn, a girl whom Rachel had lived close to in the 5th and 6th grade. Felicia had always been on the wild side a bit and she and Rachel were never really close, but they became very close during the time of Rachel's desperate need to escape Henry. Perhaps they shared the bond of male hatred or maybe just needed a companion since Felicia had been recently divorced and had a son the age of Mara. Felicia wasn't an attractive girl, being big boned with slightly thinning mousy brown hair which she wore permed at neck length. She dressed very fashionably and applied make-up to her advantage working hard to enhance the looks God had given her. She had been raised by a military father and mother and was the only girl in a sibling group of three boys. Since she had recently become a single mother Felicia appeared to Rachel to be one of the strongest women she'd ever met. They bonded on a level deeper than either of them even realized at the time and became inseparable. After several months of this relationship, Rachel became strong enough emotionally to leave Henry and on a day like every other in the turbulent, abusive relationship of Rachel and Henry, after much secretive planning, Rachel took a day of leave from work and left Henry for good, moving in with Felicia for moral, mental and physical support.

    No doubt about it, Rachel was scared, then and now. Scared stiff of Henry. Scared blind. Blind to her rights, blind to her strengths; just blind. After all she'd originally picked him to marry because of his intimidating demeanor, in size and manner, hoping he would keep her safe from all the beasts she ran from and having an anger problem, yet portrayed the epitome of quiet, playfulness and stability. The effect was terrifying. Especially since he kept his monster hidden so well from everyone but Rachel.

Aside from the fact that she had had to hide from him for 6 months until he'd cooled down after she'd filed for divorce, he'd now married a woman who, by his own confession, was twice as mean as himself. This made for double trouble in Rachel's book since this was bound to make both he and his "twice as mean" counterpart mad enough to spit fire. But so be it. The children had to come first. Rachel had had more than she could bear, not to mention the children. So, what if the court system held her in contempt for not returning those girls to their daddy at his appointed time. He'd forfeited his rights as decreed in the divorce because he'd drunk alcohol while they were in his care. And if they brought charges against her, she'd tell the judge exactly what her girls had been subjected to in this farce of an arrangement. If they wouldn't tell, Rachel would speak for them, able now to back up her beliefs with documentation she'd been advised to keep.

Little Jenny had sported a serious busted lip several weeks prior and had almost drowned, been burned, accidentally, of course with one of Jackie's cigarettes and Mara was now reporting fist fights and bouts of drinking. It had to stop, no matter what the consequences. Only.... what would those consequences be? Rachel wished she'd been braver to make things easier.

Rachel only hoped the girls wouldn't hate her for taking him out of their lives. What else could she do? She'd tried to reason with him. With both of them. Should she continue to send them and sacrifice them like lambs, letting the downhill plunge of Henry and Jackie's reckless lives possibly put them in dire straits somewhere along the line? No. Something had to be done, come hell or high water.

Rachel turned over, fluffing her soft feather pillow, trying unsuccessfully to get comfortable and go to sleep knowing she'd eventually have to tell the hot-tempered Jackie about their difference of opinion on who was actually in charge of Mara and Jenny in their future care. The thought of having words with Jackie made Rachel a bit nauseous and she climbed out of bed reaching for her robe heading toward the kitchen for a drink of ginger ale to settle her stomach. There was a niggling memory of a past confrontation with Jackie. It had been early in the marriage between Henry and Jackie. Mara had seemed distressed about her previous visit with her father and his new family which consisted of three children ranging in ages 15 through 11, to Mara's 6 and Jenny's 2. At Rachel's questioning she learned that Daniel, the oldest, had gotten into bed with Mara one night and it had scared her. Rachel assumed that since it was a new arrangement that Daniel had possibly been sleeping on the floor and becoming uncomfortable in the night, had climbed into the bed Mara occupied. Rachel was concerned, however, and made a point of calling Jackie (trying also to form some sort of relationship) to let her know what Mara had said and to make her aware that this might be something they should keep a close eye on, given the situation. Jackie had begun cussing and screaming, calling Rachel names and suggesting strongly that Rachel get her mind out of the gutter.

Rachel had thought to herself then, 'Well, maybe I'm too cautious because of what happened to me, when I was little.' And she let that be the end of that, determining to try concentrating on the good things rather than the possibility of the bad.

That was their last real confrontation. Rachel had hoped that at least Jackie would be aware of a potential problem, however and keep an eye out for trouble in this area.

Rachel sat up in bed and took another sip of ginger ale. She thought back to when she'd told her mother of what her older brother and eventually her father had done to her and how it had destroyed every bit of confidence, self-worth and innocence she could've had. Her mother, Naomi Rudd conveyed that she hadn't believed her, and the incident of the telling had pushed her into a deeper depression.

Rachel had tried to convince her mother but maybe too much time had gone by for her mother to believe her. Still Rachel couldn't comprehend the ramifications of telling her earlier. Naomi was far too fragile emotionally to have handled that kind of news then. She'd already had three nervous breakdowns by the time Rachel was 14. Rachel was 25 years old by the time she'd gotten up the nerve to tell. She'd realized then that telling at age 14 when she'd begun to stuff down the mountain of anger threatening to choke her at the injustice of it all would've been a bigger nightmare than enduring the shame in silence, alone. And so, she did just that. Rachel was trying once again unsuccessfully to stuff down the anger laced with fear and decided it was time to pray. Eventually she drifted off to sleep.

Around 4:00 am she was awake again and unable to get free of the uncomfortable feeling about the relationship between herself and Henry, even after three years and his remarriage. She kept trying, unsuccessfully to pinpoint some sort of reasons why relationships in general were so difficult for her. She thought back to the early communication between Henry and herself, wondering whether she could've done something to have made it better, especially for the sake of the children.

Early after Rachel and Henry's divorce, her Mom and Dad had given Rachel and the girls a large room in the back of their house, when Rachel first came out of hiding, after divorcing Henry. Jennifer Rose, almost two, was into everything while Mara, seemed to swing from the rafters in glee at their present living arrangements. Of course, they seemed awkward and uncomfortable to Rachel given her sensitive state of mind regarding her parents. But to the children, Rachel assumed it was safe, and it was, comparatively speaking. Still Rachel made sure it was very temporary. The money situation did little to ease her mind, however, and she'd begun to get a bit agitated with Henry for not being on time with the child support which she badly needed to compensate for the low paying job Rachel still held precariously, as it was a temporary job. Along this train of thought, Rachel had dialed Henry's number, trying to still her racing heart fearing the coming confrontation yet braving it hoping for reprieve from her current nerve-wracking situation with her parents,

"Hello," Henry answered lightheartedly.

"Hi," Rachel said, "have you sent the child support?"

"Well, nice to hear from you, how are the kids?" Henry commented sarcastically.

"They're fine, but they need the child support, so we can buy food," she returned snidely, knowing she'd rather take a beating than ask her father for a dime.

"You'll get your money." He sneered. Then Jackie, his new love interest, had taken the phone.

"What are you into this week? Preachin or smokin?" She

was obviously drunk, and Rachel didn't think a comment would be well received so she stayed silent and waited for Henry to take the phone back. When he did, his obvious drunken glee was evident in his tone as he stated between chuckles, "I found one that's meaner than me, Rachel, and she can cook!"

"Good," Rachel said with little emotion, "y'all have a good time, just send me the child support," and with that, Rachel hung up the phone.

Rachel had called his mother, her only faithful ally and questioned her about this colorful, woman, to put it mildly, he had taken up with. She had been concerned about his involvement with her and said repeatedly that Jackie was nothing but "trash and a drunk". Of course, Henry had married her four months later and then they had become a family with her and her three teenage children.

Rachel was concerned about letting Henry's visitation with the children continue in view of these new circumstances but after consulting with her lawyer found that her hands were tied. She hadn't considered the possibility of his marrying so soon after their divorce or his mate having children.

She expressed her concerns to her counselor, Grace, and Grace tried to ease her mind, but it didn't put an end to the niggling fear that began to take root in Rachel's heart from that time on. Rachel spoke with her lawyer about it, but he said, "As long as he doesn't drink around them, he has every legal right to his weekends, no matter what your personal taste is for the person he marries."

The next two years were like a blur to Rachel. She worked two jobs to make ends meet and sometimes they still didn't. Henry would pay the child support at times and at times, he wouldn't. This became a constant irritant in the relationship between Henry and Rachel. The children came home from their weekends with him, insecure and frustrated, troubled and afraid. Rachel couldn't understand whether they were having trouble adjusting to the discomfiture of the situation or whether something was really wrong. She'd question them and they'd tell her things about potentially dangerous situations they were in. But when Rachel would communicate this to Henry hoping for responsible attentiveness to the problems, she would later hear that one of their biggest problems was getting into trouble for tattle-telling on the other children. The children were bigger, obviously rougher and it turned out (Rachel had later found out) to be very jealous of Mara and Jenny and seemed to constantly have the upper hand over them. Of course, when Rachel tried to discuss her concerns with Henry, he would tell her that the girls were his concern when they were with him, and Rachel was not to worry about them. No amount of talking, threatening or begging had helped. She tried not to worry. She tried to let him share in the responsibility of raising his children. She tried hard.

The stay with Rachel's parents lasted only a few weeks and she and the children moved into a triplex apartment several blocks from them. She tried to make it attractive, but it was by far the worst place she'd ever had to live in. The shock of living in such poverty didn't wear off until they'd moved several months later.

During this time, Rachel had met a man who'd changed her life, for the better at first. She'd met him when Henry had the girls on his weekend and she and Felicia had gone out for a drink at the Officers Club on base where Felicia loved to go. Rachel didn't care, she just needed a drink to numb her tired thoughts and fears. Brent Wimbledon had played bass in the band at the club and *"looking for love in all the wrong places"*, Rachel had looked Brent's way.

The house Rachel had shared with Henry during their marriage suddenly became available due to Henry's allowing the payments to get so far behind that the bank contacted her to bring the payments current. Rachel jumped at the opportunity and after explaining the situation to the bank and vowing to catch it up, they were able to move into her comfortable A frame, three bedroom house that was situated on the one acre lot of woods that Rachel had played in growing up. She was excited about the prospect of getting the house back, but after cleaning it, refurbishing it and moving in, Rachel had a hard time making the payments and they were forced to sell after living there only a brief six months.

After the sale of the A-frame, Rachel bought a dependable, small size truck with the profit and they moved further into the woods to a geodesic dome house in a small neighborhood of domes situated in the middle of 1000 acres called Indian Skies Farmland. It was beautiful and the rent was cheap. Rachel had flourished there, as did the children it seemed for a brief time during the summer but the school was unsuitable for the children and drive was so long, they were forced to look for residence in town. Soon they had been able to find a nice little brick house with three bedrooms and grass in the yard. Rachel seemed to be about to survive the divorce and to get a grip on a small portion of a decent life. The cottage was close to Rachel's sister, Brianna, close to her boyfriend and close to the school. The girls had their own room and life was finally okay. They seemed to be a little happier, though still very troubled, and

Rachel had hopes of getting their lives on track. They started going to church and Rachel got a promotion enabling her to quit one of her night jobs.

Mara was only in third grade and Rachel had already had to take her to a psychologist. Her teacher told her she would daydream all the time and was failing in school. Jenny was still almost unresponsive, even to affection, when she'd come back from Henry's. Brianna called it catatonic and it was becoming obvious they had been getting hurt in the DeVaughns' care. Rachel started keeping a file and documented every accident as her attorney had told her to do. Like the time Henry took the family canoeing and Jenny fell out and would have drowned, had Mara not jumped out and saved her because no one was watching her but Mara. Henry had given her full responsibility for Jenny. Mara was 8, Jenny Rose, 3. Then there was the ball game where Jenny was sitting in Jackie's lap on the bleachers and fell three stairs down and busted her lip. An injury that took about three weeks to heal. That was the same weekend she had a cigarette burn on her arm, which Jackie claimed was, accidental of course.

The straw that broke the camels back, however, was the fight. Jackie accused Mara of stealing quarters out of the cash register, and she demanded Mara be punished. At least Henry had laid down the law by then about Jackie whipping the girls. Rachel saw it all so clear then. Jackie hated her children because Jackie hated Rachel, probably due to the fact that her husband still wasn't over his first wife and it was rumored that he called her name out in his sleep periodically. (He always did talk in his sleep.)

Nonetheless, Rachel had made up her mind then, she would never send them back, ever.

Rachel called her lawyer and asked if she could get papers drawn up to suspend his visitation. "Now, Rachel," he whined. "You have to be able to prove he's been drinking and an unfit parent to suspend his rights. There's really nothing you can do at this point without proof."

"Well, I'm not sending them back in that environment, even if they do hold me in contempt of court." Rachel had had all she was going to take. It was the end of this farce of an arrangement. "My children had to scramble under counters and hide to escape the violent fights those two engaged in. Mara had to get Jenny out of the store Jackie and Henry owned, on her own and into the van outside, for protection, while their daddy was choking his wife. And when she did get free from him, she threw things at him almost hitting Mara in the head with a box of Tide. Both of them were cussing and threatening to kill each other. If I can't keep my children out of this kind of environment without being locked up, then this ain't the America I thought it was. They are not going back." Rachel was appalled at the injustice she finally allowed herself to feel.

"Rachel, I understand how hard this is, but the law is the law and if he presses this, you could get in trouble. I'd hate to see that happen." Brad said, in a whiny voice that made her want to slap him.

"Thanks, Brad, but I think I'll take my chances." With that, Rachel hung up the phone, wondering why she'd ever trusted the stupid man at all.

CHAPTER 2
SHOWING THE BRUISE

The next three months since the initial break with the visitation deal had gone by with no real consequences other than a few threats from Henry. Rachel had been so braced for a fight, it shocked her that there were no real repercussions. This time of not letting Henry have the girls consisted of changes and promulgated relaxation. Treats and safety. Security and scripture. Church and family. Rachel had even begun to relax and enjoy life to it's fullest with the absence of stress over the hopeless situation that had gone on for over two years. It was time to enjoy the girls and thank God above for getting them out of that dangerous environment they'd been forced to live in. Week after week, the girls seemed to get more and more secure and more and more information came forth from them as they recaptured their bravery at not having to go back. Rachel was appalled at what her babies had been subjected to in the brawling "survival of the fittest" environment surrounding the DeVaughn home. There were still many challenges, however, such as bed-wetting and nightmares, angry fights and fears. There was an unexplained hate and fear of all men and Rachel was glad she'd made the decision to keep her girls away from his horrid influence, hoping that time and God would heal what may have harmed them.

Henry threatened her a few times about not letting him have the girls but Rachel stood her ground and told him to get a lawyer, that they weren't coming back, that he had lost them and that was that. If he wanted to see them, she'd be glad to make arrangements for him to do so, in her presence and at her convenience. He'd hung up on her and she imagined him blowing up and breaking something near him.

Rachel was surprised at the way Mara and Jenny reacted at the prospect of not seeing their father. Mara asked only once whether they were going back and at Rachel's negative response, she gave only a mild non-commital shrug and that was that.. Rachel only hoped they would not become bitter over time at having been robbed of that most important relationship but Rachel knew there was no help for it. It was better to have no male influence than a useless, harmful one.

The marriage between Henry and Rachel had been a crippling mistake from the beginning and Rachel had stupidly thought that having babies would make him into the Mister Wonderful of her hopes and girlhood dreams. Wrong. After many failed attempts at faithfulness and responsibility, the relationship had failed fatally.

Jenny's first words at age one had been stuttered and at age three, she still could not speak without mildly stuttering. She never mentioned her daddy, in fact it was hard to get her to respond to much of anything as she seemed to withdraw into a world only she could understand. She was like a rosebud that could not be opened without marring the beauty and her stem was covered with spiky thorns. Mara was like a maze of confusion. She seemed to be three or four different personalities even then. She reminded Rachel, now in retrospect, of a pinball in an active play game in which she had no choice but to push forward to the next level, and then the next until at last the player ran out of quarters and she was awarded rest.

Nonetheless, things were becoming almost normal and slowly Rachel began to relax from the gut wrenching fear she'd learned to live with since marrying Henry DeVaughn. The mornings were beginning to look much brighter.

After a good night's rest, Rachel rose earlier than usual to thoughts of hope and a light feeling about her spirit. She showered and dressed getting ready for the day. The children seemed to be unusually quiet and Rachel tried to draw them out by asking questions but to no avail. She finally just dressed them, fed them, hugged them and not having much time, left and took them to school. The day was uneventful and after collecting the children from daycare around 5:30 p.m., Rachel headed home looking forward to a quiet evening with Mara and Jenny, hoping to give them some quality time which seemed so sparse over the past two and a half years.

It was a hot, muggy, August night in Montgomery. Dry bushes and trees stood miserably still around Rachel's little cottage as the sun slunk down behind the edge of the ground only visible for a second. Not even a hint of a breeze stirred the smallest, driest, leaf. If not for an occasional car gliding quietly down the street, it would look like a still life portrait complete with pastel trimmed little houses, surrounded by greenery and plush foliage with awnings of green and white. Rachel turned from the view and went back into the house to get the girls bathed and ready for bed before reading Jenny's favorite bedtime story, The Three Bears.

"Goodnight Jenny," Rachel said quietly, as she kissed her three year old giggly, cupie doll, then switched off the light.

"Night Mommy," Jenny chimed as Rachel rubbed her forehead and smoothed her soft, clean, sable hair before walking into Mara's room for her prayers.

The night was magic somehow and Rachel felt at peace. In the three months since the children had stopped going to Henry and Jackie's house, the girls were actually starting to act nearly normal. Life was getting better. Rachel was up for another promotion at her job, the man she had been seeing for two years plus was coming close to popping the question and all seemed right with her world.

Rachel sat down on the bed beside Mara, the sunshine in her world, now eight years old, and they said prayers. Tonight was special somehow and Rachel felt inspired to quote her favorite chapter from the Bible, partly showing off and partly just trying to share her love of the Word of God. She began, "I beseech you therefore, brethren, by the mercies of God, that you present your bodies, a living sacrifice, holy, acceptable unto God, which is your reasonable service. And be not conformed to this world but be ye transformed by the renewing of your minds to prove what is that good, acceptable will of God." Rachel went on and quoted what she could and when she came to the end, her spirit rose within her and with conviction, she finished the chapter with, "And be not overcome with evil but overcome evil with good." As she finished, Mara looked at her pensively but with hope in her troubled little cherubic face as she asked, "Is good always stronger than evil, Mama?"

"Always," Rachel answered with solid faith, as she looked Mara in the eye.

"If you ask God to forgive you for doing something wrong, will He always forgive you no matter what?" Mara asked with clear determination.

"If you're really sorry for what you did," Rachel answered, "He will always forgive you no matter what it is."

"Well,..." Mara hesitated and with determination born of need she went on, " I have this friend, and if she was doing something bad with this older boy, would God forgive her, if she asked Him?"

Rachel got an icy chill up her spine and knew that Mara was talking about herself instead of a "friend", but a supernatural calm came down on her like a downy comforter, though she could never have guessed the magnitude of what Mara would tell her. Rachel continued with, "Of course, He would, if she were really sorry, but if that little girl is you, did you know that your Mama is the best friend you've got and you would need to tell your Mama." Rachel looked her dead in the eye, with a seriousness that must have looked like strength in that moment, rather than naked fear and she asked the question, knowing the answer. "Is it you?"

Mara's saucer-like, fear-filled eyes began to flood and were locked with Rachel's as her troubled face broke and she nodded ever so painfully slow. Rachel took Mara in her arms and held her sobbing body for what seemed to Rachel like a brief hug. Rachel never wanted to let go. She wanted to hold her safe, pretend her innocence was forever. After about thirty minutes Mara was able to tell Rachel some of the details.

The unthinkable had begun. It started the first night

she'd spent with her father in the house of his new family and had been going on every other weekend since. The boy was her new stepbrother and 15 years of age to her six when it had begun. ['*RAPE, HER OLD ENEMY, THE DESTROYER OF INNOCENT BEAUTY*'] Rachel thought, '*What happens to a little girl who's raped at the age of five or six? The same thing that happens to a flower that is stepped on and ground into the dirt. Until the season of warmth, new life and nurturing, that bloom remains destroyed.* **DESTROYED**'

Rachel assured Mara that God certainly did forgive her but that it was not her fault at all and for her not to worry, that everything would be all right. Rachel held Mara and lay down beside her stroking her tear drenched hair away from her face until Mara fell asleep still softly sobbing. When she was still and quiet Rachel sat a few minutes more speaking softly to God about needing real help with this and she slipped quietly from beside Mara to walk feeling like a robot to her own room in shock. A shock that would remain with Rachel for many years to come.

Rachel didn't sleep that night. She called Brent to get his wise opinion. "Of course, you know you have to report this to the authorities." He said in a matter-of-fact tone. Of course, she knew that.

"I'm so scared, Brent," she breathed. "What's gonna happen?" The fear seemed to be coming out of her pores in little invisible vapors that filled the room and threatened to use up all the breathable air. The monsters of her childhood had found her. Though she had run fast, they'd caught up with her and ravaged her helpless babies...! Oh, God...

"Bow up, now. You're made out of tougher stuff than the average mother. You're gonna be all right." His soothing tone was like a tonic and sanity tried to eventually come back as Rachel tried to sniff up tears that were trying to flow uncontrollably to be replaced with alternating fear and rage. Now in retrospect Rachel realized God must have put or allowed this man to be in her life, if for no other reason than to be a support for her during this time. She had trusted no one. There was no one else she could trust. No one. Not really even him if she were honest with herself.

THE BOOGEY MAN

Henry DeVaughn sat down at his breakfast table dragging his shaking hand over his sleep-dazed face, his raven black, shoulder-length, hair tousled from yet another restless night. His huge frame giving one the image of what a warrior chief Indian brave might have looked like in a modern setting, hung over.

The kitchen smelled of old food and scorched coffee. He drew a ragged breath and pushed up his tall frame from the table reaching for a stale beer left over from the night before. The house was silent, and he was alone with his thoughts as he washed out the coffee pot and prepared a fresh pot.

How had his life gotten so far off track? So out of his control. His wife Jackie had begun to have more serious episodes of blackouts with her drinking spells, and he'd begun to really worry about her safety, and … his own. She'd become more violent, and he thought she might end up doing some real damage to him in his sleep. She'd threatened as much. Would she really do it? He had a feeling she might. Then what? He thought he'd really loved her at one time. He knew he needed her after Rachel had left him. She'd just left for no reason. Women. Who could understand 'em? Now he'd begun to depend on Jackie too much for his own good. He now realized there was no such thing as love and if there was it was rare, and he hadn't found it. He had loved Rachel, thought she loved him, but that was a lifetime away and he wasn't sure if it was love after all. Boy, it sure did feel like something good, but he couldn't name what it really was. His little girls loved him. He was sure of that but they, too, were now gone. How could Rachel just cut them out of his life this way? He'd get even with her if it was the last thing he did. She couldn't get away with this. There were laws. Problem was, those laws wouldn't do him any good because he'd been short on cash and couldn't pay the child support required by the law, so how could he make use of those laws. Who would listen to a dried up drug addict anyway with a past and a trail? He was stuck, that was for sure and it was all Rachel's fault but she'd get hers one day. He had to just hang in there a while longer. His girls would grow up old enough to choose one day and wouldn't Rachel be shocked when they chose him over her. He could just see her hot little innocent face now, all defeated and full of fear and doubt. That's how he liked Rachel best, all quivery with fear. God, how he missed her.

He did have Jackie's kids after all. The only problem with that was, they were mean as hell and made him want a tall glass of Coors before every encounter with the little devils. Daniel, the oldest had a pleasant enough manner but he was sneaky and dad-gum if that didn't just git on his nerves.

Miranda, the only girl, was 13 and had a mean streak as wide as her mama's. She was a pretty girl with that sun-streaked wavy hair, all golden brown and freckles sprinkled all over her nose and cheeks and always slightly pinked by the sun. She's a thin girl without much womanly form, still resemblin a 10 year old not quite reaching puberty. Looks all sweet and cuddly, but that mouth. He took a tepid swig of his beer just thinking about it.

Marlon was all boy, gave you the impression that his independence could best that of a grown up, well ripened with age. His secrecy always made Henry feel like he knew something about him that he shouldn't. He was his mama's least favorite and Miranda hated him just because. So Henry felt sorry for the little whippersnapper who seemed all alone in the world and he spent many a beer pondering how to help the little fellow out.

The phone rang and skinned his brain to the painful reality of how he didn't feel up to working today but somebody had to if they were going to eat, and drink...

"Hello", he called out into the receiver he'd picked up on the third ring after bumping his shin on a full crate situated stupidly in front of the telephone table.

"Henry?" Rachel's somber question hung for affirmed response.

"Rachel?" Henry queried. Wondering what on earth she would be calling him about. His first response was to give her a piece of his mind, guessing she was wanting money again and knowing he didn't have any extra to give. The problem was, he was too shocked to think of any thing clever with which to make her feel stupid. "What is it?", he offered, awaiting her reply.

"Well," she began slowly, "I have some bad news," thinking how she would tell Mara's daddy that his stepson had been forcing his little girl into shameful acts of perverted sex. In Rachel's mind, this maniac she was once married to was about to blow his proverbial stack and her fear was that he would kill this boy, in a panicked rage. This boy who'd molested his baby girl, leaving Rachel feeling at fault for the murdered boy's wasted, hopeless life, which was about to end violently. She continued as she breathed a prayer for the boy, shutting out pictures of his bloodied body lying sightless on the ground outside his home. "It seems that Daniel has been molesting Mara and she's just now gotten up the nerve to tell it. I didn't know how to tell you other than just right out and let you know I will be reporting it, of course."

Silence,,,, and then, "What kind of !? Are you crazy?" he yelled. "That's a lie. You're lying."

Lying? What kind of an idiot would make up a story like that? Rachel wanted to know. She couldn't think. She'd gotten the wind knocked out of her sails on this call and that was a fact. Lying! This was ridiculous. She'd seen the devastation in Mara's eyes and knew this was a very serious matter of legal and emotional magnitude beyond their comprehension. This was a nightmare and Henry thought she was lying? What kind of a lunatic had she been married to for 10 years? He never even knew her. Surprise, surprise.... But if this didn't just take the cake and shove it in her unsuspecting face.

"Children don't lie about things like this, Henry," Rachel seethed, "and I certainly have better things to do than call and invite trouble like this by lying about something so serious. I'm just letting you know in advance, your little house of cards is about take flight. There's a wind storm coming. If you're smart you'll get ready." And with that she hung up.

By this time Jackie was standing beside Henry looking for all the world like a little old farmer's wife too tired in her early cow milking face to register any normalcy and as the receiver slammed down she, bellowed, "What the blazes is going on, Henry? You look as if you've just seen the capital bombed."

Henry didn't answer, he turned and headed for the door calling over his shoulder, "I'll be back in a few hours," and he strode toward the door.

"You get your ____ right back here, Henry DeVaughn, and tell me what the ____ is going on," she called out to his disappearing back and on her last syllable the door slammed with a reverberating, clash.

Henry went straight to the bar. He needed a drink and it had to have a bigger kick than the coffee he'd been sipping. He had to do some real thinking and that called for real drinking.

Rachel kept Mara out of school that morning and took her to the Montgomery Rape Center, to be directed to the Sunshine Center for juveniles. "Sunshine Center", Rachel thought offhandedly, 'to take her little "Sunshine" to.

After filling out the necessary paper work, Rachel and Mara were asked to step back to one of the offices where a counselor awaited their arrival. Rachel had no idea what was in store but she knew, like she knew nothing else, that Mara would need professional help. And Rachel was determined that she was going to get it. Not to mention that this was big and Rachel couldn't handle it alone. Rachel knew what pain this kind of thing caused. She knew first hand and knew she would need support as well.

Upon entering the office, she saw a small framed woman behind the desk, her hair was slightly graying at the temples and she wore a black suit like a man would wear. Rachel felt her heart race at the prospect of saying anything at all to this stranger about what she and Mara were facing.

"Hello," the woman greeted warmly as she stood and

gestured for Rachel and Mara to sit on the friendly sofa that took up an entire wall and she joined them at a chair adjacent to the couch. Rachel began by briefly telling the woman about the events that had led them to her. She asked if this had been reported.

"Well, no," Rachel cautiously ventured, "I wanted to contact the center first because I knew Mara would need help."

"I see," the lady pondered. After a brief pause she seemed to have a clear vision and she explained that the center was required by law to report any crime such as this, if not already reported, within 24 hours time. Rachel assured her that it was her intent to report it just as soon as they left her office and satisfied, the lady kindly told Rachel who to speak with at the juvenile division. Rachel assured her that she would do just that as soon as they left.

The lady explained that she would set up a counselor to handle the case just as soon as she had the police report which Rachel would need to bring with her to Mara's first appointment.

The afternoon consisted of a confused mass of reports and statements beginning with the initial telling at the juvenile division in a big gray building which housed a maze of various offices for Montgomery's police officers. The heat was sweltering by 10:30 am and by 1:00 pm which was the time they arrived, the muggy air had their clothes sticking to them in earnest. They registered with the receptionist and received clip-on passes to enter the division needed and after a brief description of their business, they were referred to yet another receptionist at the entrance of the downstairs offices. Rachel raked her fingers through Mara's sweat moistened hair as they walked the mazes of halls, before finding the Captain's office. Upon entering, Rachel sensed Mara's feeling of being trapped as soon as they locked eyes with the stern, broad fellow behind the desk. His chin was only slightly doubled, below a serious unsmileable mouth. He sported wire rimmed glasses that reminded Rachel of her old school principal. Mara seemed to be in shock though Rachel had carefully explained how necessary all this was but Rachel understood completely, she herself was having a hard time holding up.

Rachel stated her business and, very offhandedly, as though he didn't believe Rachel's statement, he directed them both into a back office and looked pointedly at Mara.

Mara appeared to Rachel as a tightly wound spring, finely crafted, able to withstand enormous pressure and Rachel marveled at the strength she saw in Mara's fine, smooth features. On second thought, however, Rachel thought it just might be well harnessed fear. Rachel knew about that.

The Captain handed Mara two anatomically correct dolls and asked Mara to show the position of her stepbrother in relation to the allegation. With no hesitation, Mara faced the dolls horizontally with the female on bottom. The Captain's face fell a little as he avoided eye contact with either of them. He let out a sigh that was barely audible but Rachel heard it and had to agree with his affronted attitude.

It all seemed nightmarishly surreal as Rachel looked at her little girl seeming to realize for the first time the actual severity of what had actually been going on in Mara's young life. It had been going on for two agonizing years prior, making her just six years old at the onset and stealing forever the precious innocence of a first kiss at fourteen or the awakenings of puberty and the questions of love and sex. Unfortunately, Mara wouldn't even know this for years to come. These issues would be forever twisted in her little mind unless she were to experience a miracle and weren't miracles rare? Rachel had to repeatedly hold onto her emotions to keep her sanity.

The Captain excused himself stating he would return with an officer to take a statement. In his absence Rachel reached over to cover Mara's hand as she sat passively unmoving beside Rachel almost as if she didn't dare move for fear she'd run screaming down the hallway into the free air and keep on running until she outran this horrible shame she was forced to relay before strangers.

When the Captain returned, he had a friendly black woman officer in his wake named Mable. He informed Rachel that she and Mara were to go with Mable to another office to file a report. They proceeded as Mable held the door for them to file out ahead of her.

The next room they found themselves in was a small one desk and three chair office, barely big enough to move around in. It was occupied by a tall, polite and soft-spoken Southern man with an easy smile, named Robert Kane. He took his work seriously but he didn't seem to take human fears the same way for he had a way of putting a person at ease with a simple chuckle, timed precisely at an uncomfortable time of gut wrenching recollection. Mara found herself pouring out detailed descriptions, positions and locations of the sexual assaults as Rachel held onto the chair where she was seated with a tenacious and unyielding grip. Corporal Kane was excellent at his job and though he sported a Southern hick drawl, there was nothing slow about his mind. It seemed to Rachel, this man would be cool in the fiery furnace and she silently thanked God for His goodness in allowing she and Mara to have him on their side.

There were threats made by Daniel and his mother, Jackie, as soon as Rachel answered the phone that evening when she and the girls arrived home. Daniel had obviously been questioned by Henry and was a seething bolt of rage as he blasted Rachel with accusations for not teaching her children better than to spill lies of that nature about other people. Jackie threatened suing Rachel for slander and swore revenge for this piece of work. They taunted and they raged and Rachel was in shock at the manner of abandon this boy used in addressing an adult. She finally found her wits enough to speak to Daniel, but all she could say was, "Daniel, you have done a very bad, bad, very bad thing."

His reply was more disrespectful belligerence and Rachel hung up the telephone shaking uncontrollably. Unfortunately, the phone rang immediately. It was Jackie with more threats and filthy language until Rachel felt she might throw up. Henry took the phone from Jackie just before Rachel was about to hang up the second time and instructed Rachel to take Mara to her pediatrician and then go see Lieutenant Rainey at the police department.

"Rainey?" Rachel asked stupidly.

"Yeah, do it now," he demanded with exasperated impatience, "just as soon as you've taken her to the doctor and had her examined. Tonight!", he added for emphasis.

Rachel said she would do it and hung up the phone, knowing there was no need to see Lt. Rainey or anyone else, when she'd been at the police station most of the day and had spoken to everyone necessary to ensure her of the seriousness of this matter and of their ability to get to the bottom of it.

Daniel was arrested within 24 hours of the statement made to the police. He remained in the juvenile hall delinquent center without bail until the arraignment. He was then transported to county jail to await the decision of the Grand Jury.

Rachel prayed God would have mercy on them all as she walked dazed through the next several days. She felt as if she'd put herself on auto pilot not allowing herself to break down and knowing she must stay strong for Mara.

THE GRAND JURY

The Grand Jury was held at the county courthouse 14 days after the police report Mara and Rachel had made with Corporal Kane on August 23rd, 1987. Rachel was told Mara wouldn't be needed for this procedure so she took her to school and went straight on to the courthouse. She was in full shock by this time and couldn't quite remember walking into the room full of people lining every wall at least three rows deep, only that she suddenly sat in the center of the room behind a wooden enclosure, feeling as if every one could see the hole in the toe of her three week old pantyhose. It was all very intimidating but was over very quickly after a minimal amount of questions that seemed so horribly redundant to Rachel.

Jenny's fourth birthday had arrived four days later and, simply not up to a party, Rachel took her to Sears and let her pick out a couple of toys. Jenny picked out a play dough factory and a doll and after getting her a couple of outfits and some socks which lifted both their spirits, Rachel thought, maybe things would calm down some now and go back to normal. It was not to be.

The phone rang and Rachel's heart raced when she picked it up and answered, "Hello?" her voice sounded strange in her own ear.

"Rachel," Corporal Kane called in his calm, Southern drawl.

"Yes, it's me, Corporal Kane," Rachel answered almost calming some but still on auto pilot alert.

He sounded tired. "I need you to come down to the station tomorrow and let's get Mara's statement on video, so that she won't have to keep giving it over and over to the DA and other necessary departments," he said gently.

"I'll need to check with my boss, but I'm sure it won't be a problem. What time?" Rachel answered roboticly.

"Whenever you can get here. Around 8:00 am will be good." He said sympathetically.

Mara came in then and said it was an emergency. Rachel's insides froze.

"Hang on a second, Corporal Kane, Mara says it's an emergency and she needs to tell me something," Rachel said, hiding her fear at what bomb Mara might drop now. She calmly turned to give Mara her full attention feeling like a mannequin.

"Mama, he did it to Jenny, too!" Mara gushed out with disbelieving indignation.

"Did you hear that, Corporal Kane," Rachel announced, digesting the extra shock. Leaning on this new stranger, the closest support, right then, for dear life. *Kane. Shock overload? Maybe?*

"I heard it," he announced with a deflated air. "Go in there and talk to her. Find out for sure and remember, don't show any emotion. Just ask questions and get the facts. I'll hold on." His voice seemed to be almost as tired as Rachel's mind. Rachel lay the receiver down and walked stoically to the living room where Jenny sat on the floor with her back against the couch playing with her play dough fuzzy hair barber shop. She kept her eyes downcast pretending not to notice Rachel standing there. Rachel squatted in front of her and touched her little hand, so soft, so small.

"Jenny," Rachel said softly, looking at her round little face.

Jenny raised those half inch, smut black eye lashes, displaying a set of haunted blue eyes. She didn't answer. She just looked at her as if to say, "Please don't ask me, Mommy"
.
Mommy didn't want to ask, but Mommy knew she had to ask. Rachel was careful to assure Jenny that she had done nothing wrong and that she would not get in trouble for this. The end result, of course, was that she too had been victimized and sexually dominated, which at least explained the behavioral quirks that Rachel could not figure out. Like her first words spoken being broken and stuttered. The eye twitches that had nothing to do with clearing eyesight or eye irritation. The nose twitches that had nothing to do with colds or allergies. She now understood so much more about her other problems so well.. Mara's daydreaming in school, the uncontrollable anger and territorial-ism, the depression and need for escape. Jennifer's unusual clinging, the catatonic stares upon coming home from visits with her dad. Both she and Mara's nightmares, bed-wetting and unnatural fear of the dark all made perfect sense, for the first time since Henry's marriage to his new family so closely related in time to their divorce. It all made perfect, twisted, night-

marish sense. Rachel was nauseated but didn't even have the presence of mind to throw up. She was numb. Out and out numb. Crushed. Her world shot down. Her life and that of her children in a series of acts too terrible to imagine had some twisted meaning and she was sure that she would never be able to figure it out or live with any form of dignity as she'd always desired and struggled to do.

Leaning over to give Jenny a hug, Rachel swallowed her tears and smoothed Jenny's hair with her right hand, ending the hug with a caress to her soft little cheeks.

"It's okay, Honey," Rachel whispered. "You didn't do anything wrong. Daniel did." After assuring Jenny, she would be right back, Rachel walked methodically back to the telephone and as she picked up the receiver her hand shook uncontrollably feeling the adrenaline surge her every nerve ending. With a nervous tremble in her voice, "Corporal Kane?"

"I'm here," Kane said softly, "You had better bring Jennifer with you tomorrow."

"Yes," Rachel answered absently. "I will."

The following morning there was a scheduled appointment with a specialist for Mara. Now Jenny would be video taped and examined. They would be picked up and escorted compliments of the Montgomery police.

The video taping of the girls' statements, to possibly be used in court was done and Rachel viewed the process behind a two way mirror. Her tears fell inside but she maintained her composure externally, knowing Mara and Jenny needed her to be strong, and strong she would be for they were her world.

The evening turned into another night and the night into another day. The morning wore on and all the Thanes were dressed and ready to go. Breakfast had been sparse but it didn't matter. No one had any appetite, anyway.

Rachel was clearing the table when she heard a knock at the door and her heart raced unexpectedly as adrenaline poured into her bloodstream once again. A film of sweat gathered on her upper lip, barely visible. She wiped at it while huffing in a breath and went to the door. Mara and Jenny were already engrossed in morning cartoons and Rachel wondered at their ability to just keep on functioning. The fact of the matter was, they were better off than they'd been in years and that was something to be thankful for.

Rachel called them to the door with her and opened to Corporal Kane and a female officer with blond hair and sunglasses. Corporal Kane introduced her as Betsy. He said he thought she'd appreciate a woman along for this.

A woman would have been preferable throughout the whole ordeal, but Rachel thought how kind Kane had been. She couldn't have imagined getting through it all without him either. Inside she knew her Father in Heaven had had mercy on her and positioned the best people possible to accompany her through this nightmare. Kane explained that Betsy was along for support and that she was a crime victim's advocate and an investigating officer. The DeVaughns were grateful for any and all the support they could get and Rachel greeted Betsy warmly as she followed them, girls in tow, to the black, unmarked government Grand Marquis. Corporal Kane was friendly and did a good job of keeping the mood light, trying to allay the DeVaughns' fears and discomfort. He spoke of inconsequential things to Betsy and including Rachel in his banter. It was like a cool glass of water for Rachel.

They arrived shortly at the doctors office and while Kane

and Betsy took care of signing them in and handling the necessary paperwork, Rachel sat quietly and watched Mara and Jenny looking at the toys intended to keep children occupied while waiting to see the doctor. Mara picked up a doll and handed it to Jenny for inspection giving the illusion that she were the mother of Jenny.

Finally, they were called back and the doctor was a friendly, black woman with a comforting easy smile. She held a clipboard and after reading over her pages briefly, there seemed to be a wrinkle in her brow but she quickly hid her emotion, introduced herself and asked Mara if she'd like her mother to remain in the room while she examined her.

Mara answered in the affirmative without delay.

Betsy and Kane had remained out in the waiting area with Jenny so the doctor began by asking Mara to get up on the examining table and undress, handing her a hospital gown.

"I'll be back in just a moment," she said reassuringly.

Rachel helped Mara out of her clothes and into the gown, "You okay?" Rachel asked supportively and Mara nodded without saying a word telling Rachel that she was not.

The doctor came in directly and did a pelvic exam while explaining everything she was doing and trying to put Mara at ease but Mara was showing signs of impatience and uneasiness with the whole procedure. Rachel stepped a little closer to the table and smoothed Mara's hair away from her forehead in a loving caress. A single tear streaked down into her hairline as she stared, unseeing up at the ceiling.

Rachel swallowed back the tears that threatened to come. She appeared to be the rock of Gibraltar standing strong and quiet by Mara's side, her very presence saying, "Lean on me, Mara. I can hold you up. Lean on me, Honey."

With the examination concluded and blood work drawn, Mara was allowed to dress and await the doctor's return. She sat up on the table and Rachel helped her with her clothes. Mara was buttoning her top button to her pale blue cotton blouse when Dr. Findley, followed by Kane came into the room to state her findings and Rachel, knowing what was coming, moved closer to the doctor so that Mara wouldn't have to hear the results. The doctor was of a different mind, however, and walked past Rachel, stopping close beside Mara, laying her hand comfortingly on Mara's leg. The doctor then turned her face to Rachel and said with relief, "The tests were negative. No sign of PID. Thank goodness." She let that settle and after a brief pause announced, "The damage, however, is extensive."

"How extensive?" Rachel asked in controlled panic.

Dr. Findley took in a breath and placed her hands in the pockets of her white physicians coat, then let it out slowly and with a marked arch in her brow, replied honestly, "It's hard to say, Mrs.. DeVaughn. Mara has been scarred repeatedly and the external damage is obvious, meaning she's been ripped and healed, ripped and healed. What is not so obvious, nor is it possible to gauge is the internal damage because her internal feminine organs are not even formed yet. There's no way to know for sure how the internal scarring will effect the forming of her organs when she is old enough for them to develop, but she may not be able to bear children."

"Oh," was Rachel's barely audible, unemotional, reply and she tried to remain standing though she felt she had been hit in the stomach with a two by four.

The examination of Jenny revealed no tearing and, no physical scaring.

The night came and Rachel read Mara and Jenny a bedtime story together in Jenny's room. Jenny was asleep before Rachel started on the third page and Mara yawned as her head dropped softly to Rachel's slumping shoulder.

"Sleepy, love bug?" Rachel leaned her head against Mara's freshly washed hair.

"MmHmm," Mara answered without opening her eyes and Rachel breathed in the sweet smell of her as she pressed her face close in a semi-hug. Rachel closed the book and closed her eyes, leaning her head back against the wall and trying to relax. The tension creeping up her back was like a living thing.

"Help me, Father," was her silent prayer as she shuffled Mara to bed before crawling into her own.

Rachel woke from a deep sleep, clutching her pillow to her chest and sobbing out loud with her face already wet with tears and her pillow wet as well. The pain was so intense that, she surmised, it had only been able to surface in the safety of slumber. Rachel chose to believe it was her emotions revolting and being expelled from her soul while her Father in Heaven held her. She cried on His chest, expressing all of her pain.

CHAPTER 3
THE PUNISHMENT SYSTEM

The hot sweltering day seemed cloudy but Rachel guessed it was just the fog inside her tired mind as she sat behind the wheel of car outside the juvenile detention center building where she was to meet with Mark Kaslow, the juvenile District Attorney. She turned the engine off wondering how she was going to get through yet another time of telling this truly horrible nightmarish story. She straightened her skirt while walking up the concrete walk to the large, gray building where the boy who'd hurt Mara and Jenny was being held.

As she entered the building, a cool puff of wind fanned through her clothes reminding her of the mist that covered her creases throughout her body. She took a deep breath and upon seeing a sign in sheet to her right, she stopped and looked into the thick glass encasing the office. A woman resembling a man was sitting at the desk with a cup of coffee dressed in what appeared to be a sheriff's uniform. She appeared to be bored. Burned out, probably described her better.

"I'm Rachel DeVaughn. Should I sign in?" Rachel asked, "I have an appointment with Mr. Kaslow."

"No," the woman replied, "that isn't necessary. Just go through those double doors over there and go to the end of the hall, turn left and his office is to your right."

"Thank you," she said kindly as she proceeded toward the double doors. Her smooth-sole shoes slid slightly as she walked across the shiny marble floor. She had the niggling feeling that she was about to enter the principal's office. She spied the door with the name plate, Mark Kaslow on it and took a deep breath before knocking.

"Come in," a pleasant voice called out as he opened the door for Rachel. He was a tall, trim gentleman in his late thirties. He had a kind face.

"Please, sit here," he directed and motioned to the front of his desk where two comfortable high back chairs were placed very close to the front of his desk. He sat in his chair behind the desk, picking up a file and scanning the contents.

"Thank you," Rachel answered in a confident voice that sounded foreign to the way she was feeling. A supernatural force seemed to be holding her up as she sat stiffly on the edge of the chair and mused at the comfort she felt. It was similar to the kind of comfort one receives during the loss of a loved one when the arms of God seem to be ever present for you to lean on. She sat calmly waiting for the man to question her on the grim details of this case. It had almost become a case to her for she seemed quite removed at times from the entire scene as if someone else were having this happen to them and she was merely the reporter, recapping the events.

He studied the file in silence for a brief time and asked for Rachel's signature on several statements that were already typed out and had the names of the prosecuting attorney, the intake officers who'd taken statements from the girls and several judges seals. It all looked very official and after scanning the contents it was clear that these were factual details of rapes, the sexual abuse, the locations, the frequency. And Rachel was to sign, stating that as the parent of these two minors, she was swearing that she believed every word they said, which she did. She signed it without hesitation waiting and looking expectantly to him to see if there was anything else. Mr. Kaslow leaned toward her very secretively and squinting one eye, gave a report, with pride, of Daniel's treatment in his facility. Rachel guessed he was trying to comfort her by telling her what a fit Daniel was pitching about not being allowed to get out on bail and about how the officers had left him handcuffed overnight. He went on to say Daniel's hands remained cuffed for quite some time. Rachel began to softly cry and as her head dropped, her shoulders shook lightly. She raised her head back with a determined pushing back of her emotions and looked into a face which showed surprise. But he recovered quickly and covered her hand with his deeming it normal to be beside oneself in a situation such as this. His eyes held hers as he said quietly, "Ms. DeVaughn, they are gonna draw and quarter this boy in Union Square. The district attorney is none other than Brett Niles and the attorney general, well you know our attorney general. Ralph Dudley doesn't play and has taken a special interest in this case. This boy won't get out of jail for a long, long time."

Rachel looked at him in a good bit of pain and said with an eerie calm conviction, "You misunderstand my tears, sir. This boy's life is over and he's only seventeen."

He pulled his hand away as if he'd touched fire and his

face bore an indignant shock as he asked, "Don't you realize what he's done to your daughters?"

Rachel could not have fully realized at that point the damage that had been done. She was in emotional shock, but through the pain she knew God's strength and felt it all around her. It deemed her condemnation and/or hate of any human being an impossibility.

Rachel operated on sheer adrenaline auto-pilot. She had been out of work roughly 150 hours, 125 of them were leave without pay. And she'd had to give up her secondary jobs in order to care for Mara and Jenny properly, now realizing their precarious hold on survival.

Rachel's relationship with her father at the time was not good, so borrowing money from him was out of the question. She wouldn't have asked him for money unless her children were starving and there was no other way.

As a result, her only ally was her older sister, Brianna. And Brianna became her only support outside of God, such as she was able to be. Rachel wasn't really sure how good her relationship was with Him and the boyfriend Rachel had so warmed to, became cold and unfeeling, setting up lesson drills and correcting her at every turn.

One sunny afternoon Rachel had spent the entire day trying not to have a nervous breakdown due to the added pressures from counseling issues bringing on regurgitating images of Daniel subjecting Mara to the horror that now hung over their lives like a cloud full of toxic waste. Brent was riding his bicycle through Rachel's neighborhood. While riding by her house he spotted Mara's and Jenny's bicycles in the front yard. He proceeded to hide the bikes in the bushes and then knocked on Rachel's door. She didn't feel at all like company but since it was Brent, she tried to be cordial and stepped out on the porch to see what was on his mind. He chatted about inconsequential things and then asked where the girls' bikes were. Rachel told him, but when she looked past him, it was obvious they weren't. Rachel panicked, of course, and excused herself to call the police and report them stolen. The police came and a report was filed. A few hours later, Brent called and told her he was teaching her a lesson about making the girls put their bikes around back so they wouldn't get stolen. She broke up with him that night feeling ridiculed and abandoned. She communicated to him his total disregard for her fragile state of mind and his callous manner concerning the hell she was working very hard to survive in. She knew then that he was definitely not the man she needed in her life. Not by a long shot.

Rachel had made a new friend during this time. Her name was Monique. She was the mother of a new friend Jenny had met in kindergarten. She longed to share her burden with someone but the abuse of the girls was not the kind of thing to share with a new friend, so the relationship was not close at first, though it did give Rachel some slight reprieve from the constant assault of this crisis. Rachel became closer with the girls, however, and that was a good thing. Rachel tried hard to keep her mind on the good things. "Whatsoever things are good....," and she tried to be grateful they were all alive and safe in the little cottage so sound and roomy. Though sparsely furnished, it was a home of their own.

In the investigation there were dates to remember and addresses and places. It was hard to recall because both families had moved around a lot in the last two and a half years and the memory of a traumatized eight year old was hard to follow. With the advice of Corporal Kane, Rachel had had their names changed to the last name of her first boyfriend in third grade, Brian Thane. She knew it was silly, but somehow it gave an internal illusion of a more serene time. A pure time.

The facts all came together in some form of report and the Thanes started visiting with the D.A.

Brett Niles was an attractive man with sandy blonde hair. He was sensitive, though quite adamant, indignant and well versed on his subject of the wrong he sympathetically educated Rachel on about sexual abuse and the law concerning it. He had sky blue eyes and a warm, welcoming smile. He had a no nonsense manner and Rachel was instantly drawn to his intense and tenacious strength, feeling at ease as much as could be possible under the circumstances. That was fortunate because the next several months were spent in his office under his supervision, learning about the law, the trial and the system. He was an attorney who didn't like to lose. He was like a well trained bulldog and his presence alone demanded respect and a level of trust that had been foreign to Rachel up until then. It became apparent early on that Brett Niles would become this family's knight. Rachel couldn't have known then just how much, nor the level of healing that would take place as a result of the justice seen to by this courageous, honorable and noble avenging knight. Brett showed them the courtroom and told them what to expect in the trial. He drilled Rachel until she felt like someone else entirely, not allowing herself to feel or react but merely to respond in the manner she'd been taught on every issue. Within a year of the first report, it was time for the trial.

Betsy, the crime victims' officer for the state, was like an angel from heaven. She was instructive as well as supportive and Rachel was more comfortable when Betsy was near, thanking God for her support. Rachel knew she wouldn't have made it through if Betsy had not been there to share her compassion and insight with them all. Her kindness and non condemning, non judgmental manner was like a shot in the arm to Rachel. Had it not been for her support, Rachel would have likely needed medical treatment for her pending nervous breakdown mentality.

THE PRETRIAL JITTERS

"Grace, I'm so scared, I don't think I can do this," Rachel said on the phone to the woman who'd been mostly responsible for her near sane state of mind in the previous years. Rachel thought her own voice seemed like someone else's, like she'd become this stranger that had no identity as she allowed herself to come out of the emotional shell of safety she'd hidden in since the secret was divulged. She felt like a faceless, emotionless robot, just going through the motions of normalcy. She was becoming truly numb.

"You can do this, Rachel, you're stronger than you think," she insisted and Rachel could almost see her smiling face through the phone. "It won't be as hard as you think. Won't Brianna be there with you?"

"Yes," Rachel said quietly. Rachel wanted so much for Grace to say she'd come. "I can't stay out of the bathroom, my stomach is so messed up. I really don't think I can do it." Rachel started to cry, but stopped herself, knowing that if she ever allowed herself the luxury of indulging in self sympathy, she might never get back to where she needed to be, emotionally, for Mara and Jenny. "I can do it," Rachel said quietly and she knew she would have to, somehow.

"Sure you can! Take some acidophilus for your stomach," Grace crowed triumphantly. She was so smart.

"I will. I'll do it, right now," Rachel commented, thankful for some small diversion with the pretense of fixing everything right up. "I'll call you later. Thanks," she added graciously, knowing Grace couldn't do anything anyway. This was her own thing entirely and she was just burdening Grace with something neither of them had any control over.

"Bye, sweety," she said with earnest compassion.

"Bye," Rachel returned and hung up only to pick it right back up and call Betsy. She answered the phone, "Crime Victims."

"Betsy?" Rachel questioned.

"Yes, this is Betsy," she returned sweetly.

"Betsy? Um... this is Rachel Thane."

"Hi, Rachel. How are you?" Betsy asked truly concerned.

"Oh, I'm...uh, well... I...um, what if she... I mean, I've got this... what if Jackie and Henry are waiting in the parking lot when I get there tomorrow? I have this recurring nightmare. I see them showing up in camouflage with bazookas. They do seem mad enough to try to hurt us, can we have an officer meet us at our car and walk us to the courtroom?"

"Yeah, I'm sure we can do that. Which side of the building are gonna try to park at?"

Rachel would've parked on the moon if that's where the police were going to be. So she gave her a vicinity, thanked her and hung up the phone, feeling as if she might get through this after all.

. . .

RACHEL BOUGHT an outfit for the occasion and one for the girls as well. *Thank goodness for credit cards, the spice of life,* she thought *and J.C. Penney* as she viewed herself in the full length mirror on the inside wall of the dressing room. The skirt she tried was a modest A-line plaid of camel tan and black that reached just above ankle length. The matching blouse was a black silk with long sleeves and a button up to the neck collar accessorized with a strand of white pearls. She chose a modest black pump shoe and wore soft black hose. 'Hmm', she thought as she viewed her image, 'I don't look a thing like me in all this somber black.' She looked very elegant however and the conservative outfit added to her non conservative hairstyle a blend of sable and spice. Yet, the dark circles underneath her eyes belied the effect of beauty clearly present. She decided this was as close as she would be able to get to the look the D.A.'s office personnel wanted her to have for the trial. She bought the outfit.

She'd bought Jenny a beautiful heirloom dress, pink long sleeve with a white pinafore that buttoned down the back. It fit perfect in that it was slightly on the large side and lent a frailty to her already slender if not thin four year frame. She reminded Rachel of a strawberry shortcake cream desert doll. The dress barely came to the top of her ankles and she wore white leather Mary Jane shoes with white lace socks. Her layered hair had a wispy look and reached just past her shoulders in back and laid slightly curling around her captivatingly beautiful lightly freckled face with a crop of textured bangs hitting just above her dark thickly fringed, royal blue eyes.

Mara's hair was the same length but lent her a graceful air and her dress was a beautiful tan dropped waist jumper reaching below her smooth tanned well formed calves, worn over a mid-length sleeve pink cotton blouse with a four inch page boy collar. She wasn't much on frills and it was the closest Rachel could get to frilly on her. She did want them to look their best and looking at them before leaving for the trial realized she'd done well in light of her bruised mental state. Of course fashion was always fun and it had been a pleasure to shop for this type of clothes on a needed basis without feeling guilty in spending on fashion rather than dire need. This was after all a very important event. The fate of their well being, according to Rachel's thinking hung in the balance on this event. It all seemed to come and go in a fog of clarity for Rachel. Mara wore plain pink nylon socks and tan leather Mary Jane shoes. She was a vision of sweet spirited beauty.

The day of the trial was upon them and a crisp autumn breeze brought a cleansing freshness to the usual muggy South. School had started back, so the morning traffic was a killer. Rachel had gotten an early start and hoped to bypass the bumper to bumper downtown rush. It was not to be and her hands shook as she sat behind the wheel of her 1973 green, Pacer. It had been a long grueling year and this was supposedly the climactic closure they'd all been working toward.

Rachel pulled into her designated meeting place and spotted the black and whites as soon as she turned. Her breath came out in a gush, realizing then that she'd been holding it in. She greeted the officers with a stiff smile as she got the girls out and they walked briskly up the long steps to the back entrance of the courthouse, flanked by the three officers dressed in dark blue uniforms. They carried themselves with authority and easy, wary gaits. Once inside the halls there seemed to be people everywhere. Inside the packed elevator, the smell of unwashed bodies was strong and Rachel sidled a bit closer to the officer on her left to escape the smell, shuffling the girls in front of her to stand close beside each other.

The second floor was a little less crowded but it didn't matter. Rachel hardly saw anything but a blur and haze of faceless shapes lining the walls as they passed. *Breathe, Rachel.* The officers led the girls and their mother to a comfortable holding room until time for their testimonies.

Quiet to a fault, Mara seemed to draw from Rachel's presence, a strength that neither of them knew about. They only knew they had to stay close to each other for survival. Mara placing her soft warm hand in Rachel's when she would least expect it would almost make Rachel cry, but she tried to remain strong and hopeful while inside she knew there was nothing left. "Come, God, help us", she silently prayed. "Help us stand up to this evil. Help us stand."

As they stood in the witness room preparing to come into the courtroom Rachel looked

over at Jenny who appeared to be on the verge of hysteria. Inwardly she curled up in fear that Jenny wouldn't be able to carry this off. That she would clam up and refuse to answer the questions. Embarrass us all and there would be a mistrial.

Rachel and Brianna entered single file into the crowded courtroom from the side just below the judges tower. They joined the District Attorney at the table positioned closest to the door they'd just exited. At the other of the two tables sat Daniel and his two defense attorneys.

Rachel felt the eyes of countless spectators and knew that Jackie Devaughn was among the group. She sat motionless, staring straight ahead thinking nothing other than,

"Dear God, give me strength." Brianna sat supportively at Rachel's side and when the courtroom rose for the judge to enter, Brianna's hand instinctively covered Rachel's in a rapid clasp.

As the judge sat, the court sat as well and Rachel's hand was glued to Brianna's in a desperate hold for a connection of strength.

Mara entered the courtroom looking around and seemed to be robotical in her gait as she made her way to the stand. They stopped her just before the judge and it was not in him to smile though you could see he wanted desperately to do so, giving her something to reassure her. The judge conveyed the importance of Mara telling the truth, knowing the difference in the truth and a lie and let her know that her job was simply to answer the questions honestly and to fill in the blanks trying to give graphic technical information about the alleged crime that had taken place. He explained the process briefly and then allowed the bailiff to swear her in. Her shame seemed to be enormous, yet subtly hidden for a time. *Oh, the shame,* Rachel thought, as she viewed this sweet, giving, kind and loving little creature about to answer questions about something so awful, so … Rachel couldn't think of any words to describe it. Rachel wondered if Mara, too was having some out of body survival experiences. Her strong little spirit bowed up and though she had this, 'Have I really got to answer these questions in front of all these people?', look on her round stoic Indian brave little face, she held up her hand and swore to tell the truth. Mara stood still as death and obeyed the requests of the court. Rachel thought she'd never been so impressed by anyone in her life as when Mara took that stand and looking straight ahead, answered the questions as though she was removed from the entire thing. Questions that would lock up her tormentor for good. The details were matter of fact and every so often her clear voice would crack and Rachel felt the tears stacked like an avalanche against her little hurt girl's chest. But she'd quickly squelch that hurt and get right back on track as if she were doing it all for an important mark in school. Her soul was shattered and what remained was merely a shell of the beautiful child that once was. Realizing this, Rachel slipped a little further into numbness as she watched. The numbness no one would understand. The numbness of safety and preserved sanity, hope and survival heroism.

Mara was then allowed to step down.

As the proceedings progressed and Jenny's time came to enter the courtroom, she appeared almost like a vision escorted by one of the advocate workers. The countenance on the judges face changed instantly from one of towering disgust and frustrated anger with Daniel to that of a Santa Claus as he focused on the little four year old girl entering the room. He motioned for her to come up where he was sitting in the stand area. He picked her up and sat her on his knee as he questioned her about her ability to tell what is true from what is not true. She answered every question with a wisdom well beyond her years and the judge was clearly putty in her hands as was the entire court. She soaked up the attention like a sponge and became a little impish glowworm every time she smiled. Her mischievous little face stayed focused on his every word and Rachel knew right then how this was going to go. Of course, she already knew, deep down. Something had told her in a deep, deep spiritual secret place from the very beginning that this was going to be one horrible ordeal no matter which way it went, but that God was on their side and not to worry about any of the procedure. He would be in control. A security began to grow inside her after that revelation, knowing justice would be served.

Inwardly, she cringed feeling someone staring a hole through her back. She could almost feel Jackie's eyes boring into her secretly wishing she'd had a machine gun to put an end to Rachel's charmed life. For, to Jackie, Rachel's life did appear to be charmed. She was innocently attractive. She had once been married to the man she called her own and she had two animatedly beautiful daughters. Well dressed and well groomed, well mannered and kind hearted described Rachel's little girls and it was understandable that Jackie would be envious, always wondering how she could get rid of her own little devils. Rachel supported herself and appeared to be a tower of strength and wise responsibility. If Jackie could have ruined Rachel at that very moment, Rachel felt sure she would have. It seemed everyone liked Rachel. Jackie hated her.

Upon the judge finishing his detailed questioning of Jenny, the little fairy nymph, he directed her over to the huge chair in the stand box behind the microphone looped low to accommodate her size. And as soon as she sat down and looked out, it was the first thing to catch her interest, there upon gaining her full attention and she reached up to touch it, just as the prosecutor came close, making it whir and squeal. He ignored the interruption and asked her name. The courtroom was packed and the jury sat seemingly glued to the edge of their seats upon seeing Jenny. You could almost hear the disgust of the jury for any monster who would dare do what was reportedly done to this baby. For she was indeed, a baby.

"Jennifer," she said impishly with a side cocked grin as she wiggled in the big chair and I wanted to reprimand her for not behaving better, but the judge and the attorney were pouring on the charm and she was powerless to resist their adoring smiles.

"What is your whole name," he asked challengingly and she answered in a confident tone, "Jennifer Rose Elizabeth Thane", as she became a bit more preoccupied with the microphone. He chuckled under his breath and asked a few more basic questions, making sure to position himself so that she couldn't see Daniel, trying desperately to make eye contact and inject fear into her brave little spirit. She didn't appear to have seen him up to that point and it being a crucial time in the questioning, the attorney was moving in to make his move.

Then came the first question about the abuse and the change in her manner was so visible, Rachel's blood ran cold. Her palms grew moist and her heart continued silently breaking, though she couldn't feel a thing. She was numb. Piece by piece she was falling into a steep chamber and felt as if she relaxed one little muscle, she would slither to the floor and become a pile of dust. She envisioned one of the case workers just sweeping her into a little dust pan with a whisk broom and carrying her out of the courtroom. She looked up from her musings and focused on the little face behind the microphone that had gone ashen. She began to contort as her head was drawn to one side with a nervous little stare and she could no longer make eye contact with anything in front of her. It was as if you could see into the nightmarish world she was viewing and could see first hand the pain, dominance and cruel torture of nether unreality's being so alarmingly real that she was frozen in the horror of it. Shock seemed to fall down on her like a heavy blanket on a hot day rendering the life form lifeless in the sweltering heat. The prosecutor continued to ask the questions that were causing her torment and Rachel felt the tears gather in her chest. She willed herself to stillness and watched expressionless as Jenny struggled to answer the kindly voice with the unthinkable questions. Unthinkable, yet Jenny had lived them for at least six months of her short life and maybe more. There was no way of knowing exactly how long he'd been tricking her into his room using her favorite candy and bolting the door behind them, commanding her to undress, as he did the same. The rest was inconceivable. Completely inconceivable.

Upon the completion of Jenny's testimony, the lawyer helped her out of the stand box and she was escorted from the courtroom by a compassionate advocate in a much more somber demeanor than her entrance had been. That stricken blankness in her pixie shaped face was like a flag waving at half mast and the silence was thick enough to see. The door closed behind her with a finality of the hell she would face in her poetically unjust appearance.

'This evil would not win.' Rachel swore to fight to keep her footing on sane soil. She would not succumb to this ploy of the enemy to steal her blind. She could see, would will herself to see. To see the sunshine again and proclaim that the darkness would never engulf her again. They would fight the only way they knew how to fight. God's way.

There was much ado made over Daniel's age at the time of the abuse, which seemed to be Daniel's attorney, Mr. Foxworths' main strategy. But what was truly memorable was the State District Attorney, Brett Nile, who looked so much like a savior to Rachel, she would've sworn he wore wings, a halo and sported a flaming sword. That flaming sword in the form of closing arguments ripped through Rachel's fog like a sunny day and yet tore up her heart like a jagged dagger. The closing arguments were long and full of shameful details of the abuse. When Daniel's attorney gave his closing arguments, they seemed to be shallow and without any true merit or ground. Brett Nile would await Mr. Foxworths' final word and be off and running again with another string of audacious remarks concerning the vile behavior of Daniel and the stripped innocence of these little girls. The final closing remarks made by Mr. Nile were worth recording here. They are as follows: *"All the evidence you have heard is that this man took two little girls, who I wish had had better resources available to them. Who I wish had had a father they could come to and say 'Daddy, he's doing this to me'. Who I wish could have felt something other than shame and fear and could have said to their mother, 'Mother he's doing this to me'. I wish they had had that, but they didn't. What they have is a mother who, when she finally got them to say what was happening, took them to the police. And we've got Corporal Kane and some others, Betsy Beard, who went with her to the doctor and stayed with her at the police station. We've got them. And they've got the magistrate who issued the warrants on this thing. And they've got the Grand Jury who listened to them and indicted this defendant. And they've got your prosecutor who brought these cases and presented them to you, the truth. They've got the Judge that presided and provided this forum. They've got the doctor who said yes, this child had been violated, but all of that, all of that is nothing if they do not have you.*

It breaks my heart to think that these little girls came and lived through what they've lived through here today, and relived what they have had to deal with over and over again. Please, protect our children. Thank you."

THE TRIAL HAD CONTINUED for what seemed like an eternity to Rachel. It only lasted two days in reality. The only witnesses were Mara, Jenny, Corporal Kane and the doctor who had examined Mara and Jenny. The testimonies of the girls and Corporal Kane were given on the first day and the doctor's on the second. The jury was out only 20 minutes before returning a verdict of guilty on one count of first degree rape, one of sexual abuse in the first degree and one of sodomy in the first degree. The trial was concluded with the sentencing set for April 19, 1988.

Rachel had planned a trip for Six Flags right after the trial. And after they all went out for ice cream, putting the events of the previous grueling year behind them, they did just that.

When sentencing took place Rachel would've rather been anywhere else besides a courtroom ever again but it was required that she be there. The actual sentencing came on May 10, 1988 at 8:45 am, before the Honorable Joseph D. Phelps, Circuit Judge, Fifteenth Judicial Circuit of Alabama, in Courtroom 3-C, Montgomery County Courthouse.

Daniel had yet a different attorney named John Cabot. Rachel didn't look him in the eye, nor did she lift her head much to the goings on of the courtroom activity until they brought Daniel in through a side door, chained around the waist, connecting his chained hands and even his feet as he shuffled in flanked by an officer on each side and at his back. Rachel's involuntary movement of her head raising up and her eyes being glued to his persona for seemingly the first time in a weird light caught her by surprise. She seemed to be watching the entire process from an out-of-body experience. He seemed to exude evil to her now more than ever and she saw herself look away. She vaguely heard the sentence being stated at 25 years in each case and though the bright new attorney for Daniel requested an appeal bond, it was denied. The judge answered his request by stating, "There is no appeal bond for a sentence over 20 years. I will listen to what you have got to say at a later time; but first I want you to know that if he doesn't want treatment, I want him in there just as long as possible."

A motion was filed on June 7, 1988 for Judgment of Acquittal. Rachel was not informed. She did not know what war was fought on their behalf in yet another courtroom. A war that waged for over six months and was won on behalf of the innocent in this case, keeping the guilty incarcerated, which was mild justice compared to what those little girls were just now realizing they would face for a long, long time to come.

On August 12, 1988, Daniel was appealing for a new trial based on the precept of faulty representation and the character of Rachel Thane (previously Rachel DeVaughn). Rachel's friend at the police department had recommended she change her name, to offset the argument that she spitefully made the whole thing up out of hatred for the defendant's mother after her marriage to Henry DeVaughn.

The motion for a new trial was overruled on August 18, 1988. Rachel knew of none of this activity other than that, Daniel was causing quite a disturbance in his confinement. Rachel could believe that now that she knew Daniel.

CHAPTER 4
THE AFTERMATH

Rachel accepted a few attempts at matchmaking by well meaning friends, turned down a few repeats and recouped her losses as best she could. Weeks went by slowly. Months went by fast. The children began to heal. Their relationships became more emotional and full of pain as therapy increased awareness. She made up her mind to never, trust the welfare of her children to another human being as long as she lived. Rachel's love and compassion swelled within her breast until she thought she'd explode and there were times when she'd cry with happiness just to see a sincere smile from either of them. Their lives began the uphill climb of cold hard truth and Rachel softened it at every turn. She hugged and kissed them, praised and watched them and helped them to understand a mother's love. The kind that she didn't even know she knew how to show, the kind that knows no bounds, comforts all pain and shares all hope. And they grew.

The carefree, courageous, spirited young woman who was determined to survive single-handedly, was gone and in her place was a fearful, skeptical, drained and unhappy person, Rachel hardly knew. She was used up. Purged, in shock at what had happened to them in the short year since the telling, she felt no longer useful to society. She needed someone to pick her up, she was too tired to go on.

Mara had been approved for free counseling and Rachel utilized every moment of it to the fullest. Rachel knew Mara would need a great deal of counseling. They kept every appointment and Rachel worked hard at getting this thing dealt with in a constructive way so that they could put it behind them and go on. The problem was, it was Mara who would have to do the work and after about three weeks Rachel began to notice Mara's reluctance to go. Rachel pushed and Mara pulled. Rachel insisted and Mara resisted. Rachel laid down the law and Mara broke it. The anger was becoming a physical presence in their home. This went on for the next several months and Rachel felt as if she'd run the gambit. There seemed no amount of love, listening, talking, disciplining or playing brought Mara from her shell. She appeared to have come through things all right and yet Rachel knew deep down that she'd just stuffed it. Stuffed it all way down deep so no one could see it and she became so good at it that when Rachel voiced her concerns with friends or family, they thought Rachel was the one who had the problem. The problem of letting go and moving past this huge hurt, this grueling pain became a badge Rachel began to wear. Rachel wished it'd been her. She knew that some of the trauma <u>had</u> been hers as a past victim of this sort of abuse and now as a mother of the same sort of victimization. But nothing could've prepared Rachel for the immense and impossibility of mothering this tortured child that Mara was rapidly becoming.

Everyday, Mara was slowly becoming a person Rachel no longer knew. It seemed the beautiful child Rachel once nicknamed Sunshine, because that's what Mara reminded Rachel of, a little ray of sunshine, complete with her unabashed social magnetism and optimistic personality, now lived in a world of aggressive hate and hidden anger and darkness. Rachel was concerned, confused and at a loss on how to fix it. Mara remained a closed book that had been read and discarded. Rachel had gone to every professional person she knew of to get ideas on how to help. She'd spent hours at bedtime with Mara, listening, talking, praying. Or trying to pray. She'd become confused about her relationship to God and begun to wonder if He was up there for her at all, but those thoughts were fleeting. They had to be, for God was Rachel's only hope for survival in this death of a life she now faced every waking moment and even in her sleep. If she lost faith in God, what would there be left? Nothing but darkness as it was before creation and Rachel knew more than she wanted to know about darkness. She knew that the world was dark when God started it all and had made it light. She would find a way to follow in her Creator's footsteps and turn her darkness into light. She was determined to find a way to do that.

Rachel searched out the local Baptist Church in her area and Sunday, the Thanes went to church. Rachel had set her control's on Go and nothing was going to stop her. She knew that God's light was stronger than darkness and they were going to tap into the strongest light she could find. Until she could figure out how, the local church would do.

The storm of the past several months was slowly receding and the clouds of shame seemed to diminish, or at the very least, hide, as Rachel stepped out onto the porch of her little brick cottage in the bend of the road on the quiet street lined with little painted houses and oak trees, hickory nut and pine.

"Come on, girls," Rachel called out as she held the door open and breathed in the clean spring air, looking out into the glorious, blue sky. "Thank You, God," she smiled up in the heavens and glanced back into the house to see if Mara and Jenny were coming. The girls shuffled reluctantly down the hall toward the open door and Rachel, detecting their fear to blend in the new social setting of the local church, tried to act cheerier than she felt. But neither Mara nor Jenny was stupid. They could smell the fear just like a well bred horse that knows his rider is terrified of him. They knew that Rachel, too was terrified of the new social environment they were about to enter. Nonetheless, the love that was insurmountable in all three held them together and seemed to overlook the obvious, and in silence they filed out in their pretty, fresh washed Sunday best, and got in the car with their Mommy.

It was a short ride to the church and soon the Thanes were seated with the congregation of at least 800 other people feeling more isolated than they'd earlier foreseen. And though Rachel had hoped to feel at home, she felt the opposite and like a stranger in a strange land. She looked over at Jenny as she squirmed and fidgeted with the hymnal, when seeing that Jenny's eyelashes had been cut, Rachel almost audibly gasped.

"Jenny! What happened to your eyelashes?" Rachel whispered, astounded.

Jenny never even looked up and emphatically whispered back, "I hate em.!"

She had cut them off! Her gorgeous ¾ inch long, sable

black, eyelashes, fringing the most beautiful sapphire blue eyes, on one of the most beautiful faces in existence! Rachel was baffled. What would cause her to do such a thing?

A little voice inside Rachel softly said, "She hates her rare beauty, for in her heart, it is at fault for what Daniel forced her to do to him." They'd made her feel beguiling, and though she couldn't really understand, she felt her four year old beauty was at fault. What a twisted crime this was. Sexual abuse...It was like murder of the soul. A slow torturous death.

Rachel cried inside while gently reprimanding Jenny on the danger of cutting them and made her promise never to do it again. Then she held her in her lap for the rest of the service trying to think of a way to make her understand that what had happened between her and Daniel had nothing at all to do with her beauty. That her beauty was a gift from God and that evil always tried to destroy the beauty God made. It had nothing to do with her. It was a good verses evil thing. Rachel said nothing but silently prayed, "God, help me, help my babies."

In the weeks and months to come after that Sunday, Rachel realized her seriously destitute financial situation and knew that it would just be a matter of time before something would have to happen or they were going to find themselves in a bigger mess than at present. Without the extra jobs, Rachel found it impossible to make ends meet and Christmas was just around the corner.

It was rumored that Henry and Jackie had spent a considerable amount of money trying to spring Daniel, claiming misrepresentation, asking for a new trial or appeal for a lesser sentence. As a result, the child support quit coming in and after reporting it Rachel learned of Henry's new and obscure residence. By all resources, Henry and Jackie left owing more than just child support. It was also rumored that they'd put up mortgaged property for collateral, so Rachel despaired of getting any help in that area. It seems their legal fees had exceeded $40,000 and being unable to pay, they left the state, resulting in attorneys also being interested in their whereabouts.

With Christmas nearing and the Thanes finances not much improved, Rachel signed up for help through the police department and prayed for a miracle. For Christmas shopping, she was able to only raise $20.00 for gifts. Her credit had been ruined by Henry's new wife using Henry and Rachel's old credit accounts and lying about purchases making Rachel responsible for all bills on credit and the mortgage on Henry and Rachel's modest A frame and one acre lot in the beautiful Blue Ridge Mountains, just north of Montgomery. Rachel still couldn't ask her father for help.

The day before Christmas, Rachel heard about two Cockapoo puppies for $10.00 a piece and being as far gone in her thinking capabilities as she was, not counting the cost of care for these puppies, she bought them for Christmas presents to give to Mara and Jenny thinking of nothing but The Lady and The Tramp.

The afternoon of Christmas Eve there was a knock at the door and Santa Claus entered with a bag full of presents for Mara and Jenny, two beautiful red and ivory doll houses, new clothes and assorted packages wrapped neatly in red foil and green. Rachel was so shocked she couldn't talk and just smiled through her tears as she breathed her adoration for her Father in Heaven who'd remembered her and her babies. Mara and Jenny had a modest but full group of assorted toys to play with and they seemed very content.

Santa also brought two hams, two gallons of milk, a box full of canned goods and a pound cake. It was Christmas!

After a fine meal, Brianna came by to give presents to the children and was aghast at the display she found of food and toys and clothes. They talked very little, mostly hugging and crying. Rachel could feel Brianna's reluctance to leave but knew she'd have had a harder time had God not blessed the Thane home so.

Christmas morning came and with it came the two puppies Rachel had boxed and wrapped. There was no tree but no one mentioned it and after the arrival of the puppies it all seemed to be irrelevant anyway. They were sitting on the floor in their new robes playing with the puppies when there was a knock at the door and Rachel started, wondering who could be coming by at this hour on Christmas morning. They didn't have many visitors, especially now that their world had been so altered.

Rachel went to the door and upon opening the door was in shock to see no other than Santa Claus, again. Only he looked a bit different and Rachel felt sure that this had to be a mistake.

"Um," she closed the door behind her as she stepped out onto the porch and quietly said, "There must be some mistake here," and she smiled as a perplexed look came over her gentle face and she said, "Santa Claus came last night!"

Santa was flanked by two Boy Scouts as unabashed elves and they were dressed out in their dark green elfin hats to boot. While Santa sported a large red bag, the elves carried a huge cardboard box full of gaily wrapped packages with Rachel Thane, Mara and Jenny printed neatly on the flaps. And Santa spoke quite forcefully yet jolly still and said, "These packages are all for you and your girls!"

Rachel felt giggles rise up from her tummy and she politely stepped aside for Santa and his elves. It was the most blessed Christmas Rachel ever remembered having and she breathed an adoring thanks to her Father for once again showing her His love and faithfulness for them. Rachel was beginning to believe that prayer really did work. It was a strange revelation due to the close relationship Rachel had had over the years with God.

Unfortunately, Rachel's strange landlady wasn't quite so benevolent and soon Rachel was evicted with no where to go but Brianna's, yet she knew that wouldn't last long because of the strained relationship between Brianna and Rachel. So the time came for Rachel to contact Daddy.

Though, at this point she hated all men, she swallowed her hate, sucked up her pride and called,... Mother. With Mother's insistence Daddy was willing to help and soon Rachel had purchased a small house behind the coliseum. Rachel's Dad didn't believe in renting so the house was actually owned by him until it could be paid for. But Rachel tried not to think about that and was grateful for a place to live. If Rachel's Dad was one thing and one thing only, he was a man with a heart and she knew that she'd have a home there as long as she needed one.

The house had needed some repairs and upon Rachel running into an old acquaintance she had asked him to give her a price on helping to do them if she assisted. He was a friendly man, mostly bald, with a kind face and not a tooth at all in his head. Rachel felt safe in his presence due to his kindly demeanor and jovial, yet sensitive wit and manner. The fact that his age topped that of Rachel's own Dad somehow added to her comfort for some strange reason. His name was Jake Mims and he was a few inches shy of

Rachel's 5'5" height, with a slightly bowlegged gait and seriously lined pouting face. He gave Rachel more than a price, he gave her a job opportunity working with him on Saturday's learning how to install kitchen counter tops and appliances while learning the fine art of plumbing. It wasn't long before the financial situation stabilized and Rachel was feeling some better about things in general. So when Rachel and her family continued in church and soon got re-baptized, just to be safe, Jake was there. Though Rachel had been baptized three times in the course of her child and adulthood, it seemed important to do it one more time.

With her ex gone from her life and by all accounts the state as well, Rachel began to relax somewhat and get in touch with her new friend, Monique. They had met when Rachel had lived in the little cottage but weren't able to form much of a friendship with so many pressing issues that seemed to have run through their lives like a rapid current. Now that things had somewhat improved for them both Rachel was ready for some adult socialization and not just with Jake, who was beginning to behave as if he would like to step up the relationship from friend/employer to one a bit more personal. That was the last thing Rachel considered a possibility, especially given the way she hated all men in some strange way she didn't completely understand. Rachel hadn't considered Jake a man for some reason, until he had started to act like he was interested in a more male/female relationship.

This hatred of men became even more pronounced when Rachel found that her new friend had been suffering in a physically abusive marriage and her husband was the epitome of a low down snake. He would take her head and bounce it off the floor then pin her to the wall in a choke hold as their elementary aged son and daughter watched in horror to which he would announce, "See what your mother makes me do!" Oh, Rachel hated him all right and every other breathing male on the planet. None of them were worth an ounce spit if they were burning in Hell. Rachel didn't dwell on the hate, however, and she made a solemn vow to God.

"God?" she called out one afternoon with resolution. "I'm through trying to find a Daddy for my little girls. *(She'd been taking applications periodically for five years due to the obvious need)*. I know that whatever happens, You will take care of us and meet our needs whatever they might be." That prayer seemed to be one of those that broke through the golden floor of Heaven and reached the singing ears of cherubim and seraphim alike, because something inside Rachel rested. That prayer evidently was predestined supernatural faith because even though she wasn't a horrible person, she wasn't exactly living the lily white Christian life either. Yet in a very brief time she met the man who would change her life forever. She would meet her soul-mate.

CHAPTER 5
THE THERAPY

Rachel had been divorced for five years by this time and had casually dated enough to know that there were no good men "out there". There was no use trying anymore to find one because they didn't exist. She resolved herself to the single life and hoped for the best, though her morals were in a state of disarray and being raised as she was, she believed that going out dancing was just one of those things people did, Christian or no, and she began to build a social life.

Monique and Rachel had became friends right away. She was tall and graceful with warm brown eyes that seemed to laugh almost all the time as her wit and humor could have charmed the saints and as she talked about her life it seemed that she had the perfect husband, life and relationship with her kids. It was only a short time before the truth revealed her tormented life and after much talking, confiding, abuse shelters and separation, her marriage met it's rightful death.

On the eve of Monique's divorce finalization, some girls

from Rachel's office came out with Monique and Rachel to celebrate by going out dancing with them. Rachel felt sure they were all due a little fun, especially herself and she planned to have plenty. Mara had been dumping truckloads of anger on Rachel and thought it only natural to let it out on her since Rachel was the safest and handiest dumpster around. However, being a neglected child herself, Rachel really took a beating during this time, emotionally, and found it difficult to bear the entire burden of what her life had become. It seemed out of control and certainly not the life Rachel had dreamed she would have one day. Especially since one of the reasons Rachel wanted to have children in the first place was to have someone to love her. She saw how mean and negligent her mother had been to her. Yet, Rachel had still loved her mother. How much more would Rachel's children love her if she were a good mother? She felt sure her own children would applaud her, since she planned to do a much more superior job than her own mother. Nobody told Rachel the impossibility of being what you'd never seen, had or known. Rachel had had no pattern to go by, no role model to copy and no real chance of having what she most desired: to love and be loved. Any kind of love would've been nice. There was a passel full of "real" men that would've liked to pretend for a little while. Rachel had an intermittent flow of contestants going for the gold and yet, she saw the emptiness in every heart she searched. She knew in her own heart that she couldn't date one more guy, she couldn't hope one more minute that she would find a good man to help her raise her two, now fragile daughters, and be the father they so desperately needed. Oh, how they needed a man's love in there lives! The right kind of man. The damage done by the thief of their innocence had marred them, but the trauma became a deep and long lasting wound with Henry's rejection of them by his not believing their testimonies about the rape and repeated sexual abuse. Rachel recalled again putting her faith in God several weeks back and praying, "God, whether I find the right man or not doesn't matter anymore. I know that You'll take care of us, no matter what," and she had, knowing from her church affiliation in childhood that grace was free and you couldn't earn your salvation so you might as well enjoy yourself to the fullest. That's the way Rachel saw it then anyway. Little did she know, in her carefree abandon that in a very short time, she would meet the precious lump of clay God would use to teach her about a lasting love she'd never known existed, an enduring love depicted only in the movies and a completing love that would last a lifetime, healing the pain of her tortured past and bringing the beauty and joy of heaven into her present.

THE GIFT

Two weeks had passed uneventfully and the girls seemed edgy for some action. Rachel thought she'd see if they wanted to spend the night with their Aunt Brianna. They always loved going over there and Brianna had called to see if she could keep them for the night and maybe take them to her sons base ball game the next morning.

"Mara?" Rachel called out the back door where she and Jenny were playing with Shalimar, their new yellow lab puppy.

"Huh?" Mara came running up out of breath, "What cha want?" she asked between two gulps of air, looking back over her shoulder at Jenny rolling around, avoiding the licking puppy searching out her face.

"Oh, I was just wondering if you and Jenny would like to spend the night with Aunt Brianna."

Jenny, having heard Aunt Brianna's name, jackknifed up and catapulted toward Mara and Rachel squealing excitedly, "I wanna go Aunt Brianna's house!"

Rachel chuckled as she shuffled them inside, reflecting on the display Jenny always seemed to make. She seemed to have created the phrase; "So full of life."

Rachel got both girls bathed and dressed in fresh clothes before packing their overnight bags and dropping them at Brianna's house only a few miles away. On the ride back home she thought of the nice hot bubble bath she planned to take.

While soaking in the bubbles, Rachel thought of Jenny, her age, and wondered if she herself were like her at that age, but try as she might she couldn't recall her own age eight. She sat up and stared into the shower curtain trying to get a glimmer of a memory but it was a blank. All she could see was her brother, seven years older and a hall, a long dark hall. She realized suddenly that the water had grown cold and she wondered how long she'd been searching down the halls of memory lane. She got chills trying to bring lucid memories from that age, that Jenny was now and it brought an unpleasant memory Rachel couldn't define. *Why could she not remember?* She thought as she ran more hot water and settled down deep in the blanket feel of the luxurious bubbles warming nicely now and she turned her thoughts toward what she planned to wear for the evening out with her friends. Her dress was casual and made from two different color T-shirts with red at the top creating a drop waist effect and the bottom a turquoise blue with a pocket of blue contrasting the red at the top. She'd chosen a cute little leather sandal that accentuated the style of the dress and she knew she would be comfortable and attractive since she'd only recently had her hair done in a style that fell free in loose curls down her back while the top was spiked and blond. She pondered the attention she might get and resolved herself to sticking close to her girlfriends rejecting all male attention, which wasn't hard since she detested the rotten snakes anyway.

The phone rang reminding Rachel that she was supposed to call Monique as soon as she had gotten home and she knew before answering who it was. She jumped out of the tub dripping with bubbles and grabbed the phone on the fourth ring.

"Hello," Rachel said as she sat, wrapped in her towel, cross legged on the bed with the receiver pressed to her wet ear.

"Heeelllllooooooo," Monique purred into the receiver.

"Oh! I'm sorry I didn't already call. I jumped in the tub," Rachel responded with a smile looking forward to spending the evening with her friend. "You ready?"

"Yeeeesssss, you wanna just meet at the club?" Monique offered softly.

"No, honey, I'll pick you up in about an hour. Okay?"

"Okay, sweety, I'll see you then." Monique seemed to be pleased by the fact that Rachel would be picking her up.

"Bye, Monique." Rachel said comfortingly.

"Bye," Monique said and hung up.

The ride to the club was somewhat quiet. Monique seemed to be in as pensive a mood as Rachel suddenly found herself in, somehow. But Rachel knew that everything would change after Johnny Walker Red made the scene.

Rachel and Monique were both feeling considerably

lighter after sharing their table with Johnny Walker for a bit and were enjoying the company of their girlfriends. The show wasn't bad either and consisted of a team of muscle-bound male dancers. Monique and Rachel had a carefree time with lots of laughter and girl talk. It had been quite a while since they had really let loose and thrown caution to the wind, abandoning their inhibitions. The invitations to dance became numerous after the show and Rachel had grown a little winded. She was prepared to sit back and enjoy the music for a while, indulging in her favorite pass time, which was watching people. People fascinated Rachel and amused her. She could spend hours doing it and was enjoying herself very much not noticing that she had turned down several invitations to dance and was alone at the table. Behavior of human beings had always been a good tool of education for Rachel and she sat there pondering this when the face of a gorgeous man came into view with a casual smile riding his polite expression. He actually looked too beautiful to be a man and looked very much like a movie star, with the eyes of an angel. He looked too good to be true and he held a questioning look on his handsome face appearing to ask, "Would you like to dance?" Rachel thought she might be seeing a mirage and had to blink, twice. His hair was mostly covered with a baseball cap but Rachel could see the silver behind his ears, though he was unmistakably young. Late twenties, she'd guessed, and she noted his cowboy boots with an amused interest. Her gaze ventured back upward and locked onto the most seductive sky-blue eyes she'd ever seen. The tan on that face had Jamaica written all over it.

He seemed to be smiling on the inside and he didn't seem to say anything as he patiently stood awaiting her reply to his unvoiced question. Rachel had really done all the dancing she'd cared to do, but one look at that face had her sliding back her chair and staring into his eyes as though she were hypnotized. Rachel couldn't believe it. He was clearly Hollywood material and her skeptic antennas went way up. *There are no men like this in Montgomery*, she thought, *they all live in Hollywood, make T.V. commercials and drive $90,000 cars.*

Though she liked the song he'd chosen to dance to, the music seemed bland in comparison to his silent charisma and she was undeniably bitten. Only it was like a mosquito bite. You don't know he's got you 'til his bite is well under way.

After the first dance, Rachel drifted back to her seat and felt she needed to pinch herself but realized it was probably a fluke or maybe Johnny Walker had hung around a bit too long and that'd be the last she'd see of this gorgeous man anyway, leaving her forever daydreaming about the most beautiful man on the planet.

As bitten as she was, she refused to allow herself to believe it or feel it and she shrugged it off as if it were a fine fur some rich dandy had gifted her with and she found it too burdensome to wear.

Monique was oblivious to the world outside as she laughed with a Chippendale dancer look alike and drank in his very generous flattery. Rachel thought Monique was due a little excess in that department and Rachel wouldn't have been a fly in her ointment for anything. Monique was glowing.

Rachel was lost in her thoughts and the heart-pumping western music played by the soulful young band, when that honey-sweet voice, complete with southern drawl closed the space between Rachel's guarded ears and the perfect stranger's sensuously confident mouth, "Would you like to dance?" he asked,

Oh my gosh, she thought as she conceded by pushing back her chair and following him to the dance floor determined to turn on the dance light and see just what he was made of. He seemed unaffected by Rachel's intoxicating beauty as most other men had been in the past making stupid comments that were transparent and fumbling over themselves setting seductive traps.

At the conclusion of the dance Rachel was more confused than ever about this quiet, confident young man. After catching her breath and pondering on several possibilities about his origin and nature, he appeared again.

She was floored. And if it were possible he was more beautiful than she'd recalled. He seemed to be surrounded by a soft light. She decided right then to cut back on Johnny Walker and drink water. He was too good to be true but there he was again. Rachel hesitated slightly and rose to her feet with a coolness she didn't feel. As a matter of fact, the room was getting warmer and warmer.

The dance was slow and their bodies swayed to the sound of the sultry country song. Rachel's heart was racing and her breath came slow and soft almost as if she knew that breathing too deeply would break the spell. *This is a bit much,* Rachel thought to herself. Her suspicion and curiosity reached an all time high because after all, men were jerks. All of them. This much she knew and she was not about to fall for one of those jerks, oh no, not Rachel. She'd learned her lesson. She didn't care if he did look like Paul Newman. There had to be a flaw, a big one. Probably in character or a wife and ten kids with a continuous bottle of whiskey to give confidence to his oh, so ready fly.

"What's your name?", he asked close to Rachel's ear and his silky southern drawl tickled deep inside her. *Oh my gosh, what is happening to me?*

"Rachel. And yours?," she gambled cautiously, squinting up her face in trepidation, yet unable to resist his subtle tenacity. *"I refuse to get swept away,"* she reminded herself sternly.

"Heath Billings," he answered easily.

"What kind of work do you do?", Rachel ventured quickly.

"I'm a roofer," he said simply and Rachel's heart melted a little. *He works very hard*, she thought, *usually hard working men are fairly good men. Aren't they?* she reasoned internally. "That's hard work. Isn't it?" she asked softening her senses.

He just kind of smiled and shyly nodded his gorgeous head.

Without realizing it, Rachel relaxed against his warm body and let the music soothe her soul. The effect was intoxicating and she found herself getting all starry eyed in spite of herself. "You sure don't look like a roofer," she smiled.

"I don't?" he questioned evenly.

"No," Rachel answered honestly, "you look like you might be a Chippendale dancer. Are you?"

Heath laughed quietly and smiled lighting up Rachel's sky as he slowly shook his head, clearly amused. *It's like he's magic or something*, Rachel thought, *like I have no control over my own mind.... and soul.*

The silence made Rachel nervous and she had to break it, "You probably could make more money as a dancer. You sure you don't dance for Chippendale's?" Her eyes went involuntarily to his chest where his shirt was opened an extra button and she feared she'd put the heat on hotter than at first for she could feel his eyes following hers. Time seemed suspended and when Rachel looked around, dazed, she realized they were alone on the dance floor, the song having been over for longer than Rachel knew and Heath didn't seem to care. She looked up to his face, to those eyes that held hers every bit as soft as his arms still held her body. Rachel had the unshakable feeling he might really be an angel.

With a deep breath that she felt in desperate need of she pulled away and embarrassed, Rachel slid her hand down his arm to take his hand so they could begin their descent to the table she'd shared with her friends. Upon touching his hand, she stopped and turned to look at him as if it were the first real look. She felt that her heart was knit to his in a way she could never have understood in that moment. She only knew that they were connected in some other universe than this one. One that she'd only dreamed about when she was very young. She thanked him for the dance and announced to him that he was coming over to meet her friends.

When Heath and Rachel arrived at her table, Heath seemed reluctant to leave, so Rachel asked if he'd like to join them. At his pleasant nod, Rachel made introductions and it was obvious he had captivated the rest of the table just as he had Rachel. His beauty seemed so uncommon in a man and a rare find, bringing curiosity to the surprised group at large. His charisma seemed to bring an enlightened presence to the other three women at the table. As the night turned into morning, Heath and Rachel stayed as close as a man and his money, a mother with a newborn or a new found prize. It seemed to be more than love for both of them.

Parting was more than sweet sorrow, it was a physical pain for Rachel and when the time did come, good-bye was said too many times to count with the soft caress of lips touching, bodies blending and feelings of desire too strong to ignore or calm. There seemed to be electricity all around them, urging them onward toward unity, completeness and serenity even as early as this first meeting.

Heath had given Rachel his room number in the hotel where he was staying when they had parted and it had been burned in Rachel's mind. On rising the next morning, that information was her first thought and after only three hours of sleep, she found herself dialing his hotel and calling out that number to the hotel clerk. *Maybe she was just trying to find a flaw or maybe just unwilling to believe that the goodness she sensed in this man could exist and was determined to expose him for a fraud.*

At 8:00 am, Saturday morning, Heath's hotel room phone rang and the greeting with which Rachel's sultry voice touched his ears had a warmth he hadn't know possible. He was beyond captivated already, but it now seemed to him that they were destined to be together.

"Would you like to go to a movie tonight?" he asked, raising up on one elbow.

"Um, I'd like to ," she answered disheartened, "but I promised Mara and Jenny, that's my children, that I'd take them skating tonight. I guess we could drop them off and catch a movie close by. How's that sound?"

"Yeah, we can do that. What time do you want me to pick y'all up?" he asked expectantly and beginning to wake up in earnest.

"Why don't you just meet us at the rink around 7:00 and we can go from there," Rachel offered and she gave him the address.

"Oh, okay," he conceded, "I'll be there."

Rachel could not have known the pleasure Heath felt at her invitation to meet for his manner was guarded as he had grown accustomed to doing when dealing with any new person, especially a female.

Heath Billings was a quiet, country boy who worked for his father in the family business and was just looking for some company, someone to socialize with when he'd asked the front desk clerk at his hotel, where he might find a quiet country bar to have a beer. He'd not been looking for female companionship. His life was already complicated enough with his ailing father and the large family his father's business supported. At that particular time, however, things were going fairly well and he had had a brief window of opportunity to catch his breath. He'd seen Rachel and her friends and had become so effected by the sight of her that he couldn't seem to see anything else. He'd never seen a woman so perfect, from her blonde hair, complete with flowing curls down her back and bangs haloing emerald green eyes to her sun-pinked cheeks and graceful feminine gait. Her trim curvy form was fitted in a red and blue cotton dress giving the illusion of gliding above her tan sandled feet and painted red toenails gracing her small smooth feet. He hummed to himself as he groomed for the evening and wondered how he'd found himself about to date a woman with two kids. He'd always told himself he wouldn't want to date a woman with children and yet his curiosity had spurred him on. Most of the girls he'd had contact with were usually intimidated by his looks and therefore seemed on edge or clumsy or very transparent in their quest to capture him. He'd regularly felt like a door prize at a women's tea or some other silly female social activity.

Rachel, on the other hand, was a very warm and unpretentious woman, very beautiful with soft hands and an honest smile. This night he would be able to tell what kind of person she proved to be. You could always tell a lot about a person when witnessing their interaction with children. He planned to pay close attention. He couldn't stand the type of woman who tried to own him. Bossy and arrogant women who try to get their hooks in a man and suck the life right out of him. He'd heard the talk and he wanted nothing to do with that type. If only women would be themselves and be honest, satisfied with the hand of fate. "Women," he grunted, shaking his head, "who can understand 'em? Not me. Maybe this one is different," he thought. She sure didn't seem like anyone he'd ever known.

"Hey," Heath's brother, Dewayne, called lightheartedly from the open doorway, "Where you goin' all brushed up?"

"Got a date," Heath answered as a smile moved slightly over his face and just as quickly went away.

"Oooowee," Dewayne teased, "out only one night in three months and you done found one worth spendin' some money on, huh?" and he poked Heath in the ribs trying to get more response. "What's her name?"

"Rachel," Heath answered squirming away from the poke Dewayne had given him. He ran the brush through his blow-dried hair getting out the unruly wave that tended to bump up at every turn and finally getting it to a semi-calmed state, reached for the hair spray to keep it there.

"What she look like?" Dewayne asked playfully, "How old is she? What ya'll gonna do? Go to the drive inn?"

Heath looked at Dewayne with laughter in his eyes. "Why all the questions?" Heath asked playfully. "You writin a romance novel?"

"Just curious," Dewayne laughed and seemed to be seriously expecting answers to every question.

"Well," Heath looked off distantly and began recalling Rachel's persona as if it wasn't burned in his brain. "She's about 5"4", blond streaked hair, pretty and we hadn't planned on the drive inn. Oh... and uh, don't wait up for me, I'll be all right in case you're worried." Heath smiled at Dewayne and left him with a smirk.

Heath arrived at the skating rink just as Rachel was getting back in her car and she motioned for him to join her. He parked and walked casually up to the car, "Hey," was all he could say. Her smile was too warm, her face too innocent and her eyes too honest. He felt his palms getting moist.

"Hey, you ready?" she asked and her voice reminded him of classical music. he nodded and smiled but stood still until she spoke again.

"You wanna go in my truck or yours," she asked.

"Whatever you want to do," he answered as he thought how warm the August night was getting and how her skin seemed to glisten at the front of her throat and upper chest that was slightly exposed over her v-neck shirt.

"Let's go in mine." Rachel offered and they were soon on their way.

After some speculation about missing the early movies which started at 7:00 p.m. and being too late getting the kids if they went to the 9:30 showing they decided to just drive to the store for a soft drink and parked close to the rink to talk in the truck.

Rachel didn't believe in love at first sight until then. She didn't know if he did or not. He was beautiful and so strangely familiar. She thought at any minute she would awaken to find him just a dream or just as nasty as every other male she'd ever known just tricking her.

They sat in the cab of Rachel's snug little Mazda B2000 drinking Coke and enjoying being together. They talked about the usual things and Rachel ended up talking about movies. Heath listened and asked questions but otherwise never interrupted listening intently as she described an entire movie to the point of Heath being able to almost see it. He was entertained both by Rachel's ability to retain and relate an entire movie and by the way her eyes shone in the moonlight lighting up his world.

They were virtually inseparable after that night except for work and sleep. Their second weekend together, Rachel suggested a trip to their family's lake cabin for some swimming on Saturday. Jenny was totally taken with Heath from the beginning and while swimming around, asked if he was going to marry her mother. Rachel was mortified with embarrassment over Jenny's obvious aggression and scolded her gently while treading water to stay afloat.

"Jenny," Rachel admonished, "you shouldn't be so forward, honey, you don't know but what Heath is an ax murderer!" and Rachel tried to look serious although she had to admit the thought was unbelievable for anyone who had any judge of character to look in Heath's face and see anything other than sincere honest nobility.

Jenny looked at Heath mischievously and replied surreptitiously, "Unh unh, I bet he don't even have a knife. Do ya?"

Heath gave his most intimidating stare as he fixed his eyes to hers, round with excitement and nodded his head slowly as if to say, "You better listen to your Mama and mind your manners, it's a big world out here and you better stay close," and Rachel fell a little more in love with him.

After a bit more swimming Rachel and Heath left the girls in the water while they sat up on the patio and watched them play. The conversation somehow turned to marriage, past and future. Heath popped the question that both shocked and scared Rachel.

"Would you have another baby?", he asked seriously.

Rachel's heart seemed to have control of her brain and she heard herself say, "Yes."

His apparent satisfaction over her answer shone in a smile that made Rachel's stomach feel full of butterflies.

After only two months of dating, Rachel was swept away in the throes of a love she'd never known and had fully believed would never come to pass for her. Heath was warm and present, attentive and stable, serious and yet, light humored, seeming like a sheltered child, untouched by life's crudiments and ploys of destruction.

He was equally mesmerized with Rachel and thought her to be some fabrication of his imagination, too good to be true. He was attracted to her trim beauty and innocent, hopeful, pleading eyes. He'd drowned in them even when just recalling their times together talking, laughing or relaying events of the day, when she would look up at him with every emotion in her heart as if to say, "Every word you say is vitally important to my future. I respect and desire every particle of your essence." He recalled her bright conversation and felt instantly grateful to God for putting this ray of light into his days, praying that He would let him have some nights as well or maybe all of them.

The days weren't long enough and the nights flew on hummingbird's wings seeming to never get close to the time

Heath and Rachel craved of each others company. Rachel began to get the feeling they were keeping too close company for the children's sake if Heath didn't have it in his mind to make the relationship permanent. She had always tried to live morally before her girls and keep them sheltered in regards to Rachel's dating relationships. She knew that with Heath spending so much time at their house, Mara and Jenny would be effected were this not to be a permanent relationship. They were all three feeling as if Heath may have been the answer to all their prayers. After Heath's visit one evening in November, Rachel decided it was time to either back away or go for broke and she put the dilemma to Heath.

DECISIONS

"You know, Heath, um, we've been quite close for a while now and don't get me wrong, I want you here as much as possible but if this relationship is not going to lead to a permanent one, it's probably time we cooled it some. Maybe start practicing some distance. Not that we couldn't still be friends or whatever but .... you know what I mean?" Rachel queried.

Heath never faltered and silently digested Rachel's little speech, making his decision for permanence known by going to the sink and filling the coffee pot with water, making coffee and then going into the living room where he pointedly sat down on the couch. Looking up at Rachel with those beautiful big blue eyes he motioned for Rachel to come and sit down beside him. All the while he sported a mischievous little grin that reminded Rachel of a little boy who'd secretly hidden a frog in his pocket unbeknownst to his mother who'd cautioned him against bringing the horrid creatures into the house.

Plans were made that month to marry after Christmas and Rachel thought all their problems were surely over. Euphoria seemed to have found her and she'd found her knight in shining armor. Together, they would win this war. This war that seemed to be Rachel's but she felt sure effected everyone in different ways and at different times. The war for good to triumph over evil in the form of eternal love. They had a bona fide family now and the problem days were gone. She just knew they were.

THE WEDDING

Heath was a very simple man, even if he did resemble a mix between a young Paul Newman, Elvis Presley and James Dean. Him being a simple man, Rachel thought it fitting to have a simple wedding. The details were discussed and cheerfully finalized in one phone call to Heath's mother. The wedding would be at her house; the house that brought Heath to manhood. She would also bake the cake, arrange the flowers and supply accommodations for all who needed them, since Rachel's residence was roughly two hours away. All Rachel really had to arrange was her dress, Heath's outfit, the girls dresses and honeymoon plans which consisted of chalet reservations for three nights in the majestic Ozark Mountains of Tennessee.

Rachel's dress was candlelight satin with a choker collar above a romantic rose patterned lace chest and back inlay of the same color. The gown was tea length with a large bow and train. She wore drop pearl earrings and a glow that had to have envied the angels. She had never been happier in her entire life and for the first time she could recall, she felt normal, whole and loved; a rare group of feelings indeed.

Heath's siblings, six strong seemed to all take an interest in making this wedding special. The youngest brother, who reminded one of a lumberjack on first sight, escorted Rachel down the walkway through the middle of the house into the dining room which had been made to resemble a banquet hall with chairs lining the walls. The brother closest to him in age and looks was the Best Man. The oldest sister, just two years Heath's senior supplied the wedding foods, drink and goblets, the youngest took pictures and the middle sister tried ineffectively to keep toddlers satisfied throughout the somewhat lengthy ceremony. Rachel's sister, Brianna and best friend, Monique, stood as her Maid of honor and Bride's maid. Brianna was dressed in classic green and Monique in royal blue satin. Mara was a bridesmaid and was radiant in lavender satin. Jennifer wore pale blue and looked more like a flower than a flower girl. In attendance along with Heath's parents and the wedding party were their mates and children, Rachel's little brother, Luke, his wife, Catarina, and their three children, Jeremiah, John Paul and Angelina, Heath's grandfather, Edward, and Monique's two precious children, Wilds and Shannon.

The wedding was magic and everyone who witnessed it knew that it was. These two people seemed so uncommonly perfect together, it was rather surreal, yet reality was the intense magic of this unusual perfect love. Heath and Rachel both were fearless in the face of a hope neither had ever before experienced and unbeknownst to the other each was terrified for different reasons but it was hidden so deep, even they did not realize it was there. They both saw a supernatural hand in this especially since Heath had invited

God into his heart during the counsel before the wedding by the preacher, Dan Bellows. "It was the right thing to do," Heath had said to Rachel when he joined her in the car where she'd been waiting for him.

First love, first hope, first true unfaltering faith in a God who truly did love and was waiting for opportunities to bless those who were learning to trust him. Heath threw the garter, Rachel tossed the bouquet, they left in a shower of rice and embarked toward three nights and four glorious days of their honeymoon. A time of eternal hope and fusing oneness described it perfectly. They fit together like nothing in their lives had ever fit and they were both filled with a mystical wonder at their future.

CHAPTER 6
THE RELIVING

While the relationship between Heath Billings and now Rachel Billings was as close to perfect as either of them had ever known, their family problems were only just beginning.

It had been less than a year since Daniel's sentencing and he had already appealed, which meant that Rachel would have to go to court and answer questions. This terrified her in a way she couldn't describe to anyone, not even herself. Of course, Rachel had told Heath all about the case and how devastated they all were by it. And Heath, along with Rachel believed it to be over. They were both wrong, and with the court appearance Rachel had to make, he watched her change from the hopeful beauty he'd fallen in love with, to a terrified shell of a childlike soul with shock written in her eyes like a photograph plastered on her fear-filled face.

Heath and Rachel arrived at the courthouse and she squeezed his hand as they walked into the courtroom where the proceedings were held. They sat down and waited for

Rachel's name to be called in the midst of all the other cases present and though she looked all around the courtroom, she did not see Daniel. After a final sweep of the room, the door in the back swung open and in walked two guards with Daniel shackled between them. His hands were cuffed and attached to a chain around the waist of his shapeless orange jumpsuit. His jaw was set and it made Rachel shudder uncontrollably inside as she squeezed a little tighter to Heath's already suffering hand. *It's a good thing Heath works hard with his hands.* Rachel thought. Heath tried to lend what comfort he could by cupping his other hand over the two that were clasped tightly together.

Daniel was brought before the judge's stand and Rachel couldn't hear what they were talking about. Her name was called after several moments and she walked alone up to the stand where Daniel stood, still flanked by the guards. She seemed to be having an out of body experience and couldn't recall how she'd gotten up there, but suddenly there she was and trying desperately to keep her knees from buckling as they were threatening to do. She stood erect and didn't know what to do with her hands, finally lacing her fingers together to keep them from trembling so, when she realized they'd asked her a question.

"Do you feel that Daniel should be incarcerated for the crimes he was found guilty of on January of 1988?" Helen Stone was asking Rachel.

"Yes," Rachel answered thinking that was a stupid question.

"Daniel feels that his trial was unfair and that you coerced the girls into lying on the stand. Is that true?" Ms. Stone asked.

"No." Rachel answered smoothly though her resolve

seemed inwardly shaken at the possibility of a new trial or his release.

"Thank you, Mrs. Billings. That will be all. You may be seated," the judge directed and Rachel returned to her seat.

Judge Phelps then directed his replies to Daniel and Rachel heard him say, "Appeal denied. Sentence stands." He hit his gavel stood up resolutely and left the courtroom as the guards pulled the stunned prisoner along toward the door they'd only recently entered from. He shot Rachel a murderous look over his shoulder.

It wouldn't have been fair to say that Rachel was not effected each time she had to think about Daniel or see him. She wasn't quite prepared to know exactly how to feel about it all. She knew he'd done a most horrendous thing and yet she wasn't comfortable standing in judgment over anyone. She felt very sorry for this boy's wasted, and twisted life. He was an attractive boy and could most likely get the attention of almost any female he chose, yet he'd chosen, a child. Rachel was baffled, she was downright confused how someone could do this to an innocent, knowing it would steal their very soul away from them. What kind of heartless animal would do it? She couldn't fathom the heart so cold that would do such a thing, but she was learning fast that mankind was capable of terrible greed, selfishness and insanity. Rachel chose to leave it in the hands of the system, however, and keep her focus on her children where it belonged. She couldn't afford to think of anything else. The laws were made to protect the innocent and though it hadn't protected them as such, it had sought and served justice. It had been an unfortunate thing that had happened to them, but it was over now and Rachel tried to let it be over. It was easier said than done.

The Billings had settled in to blessed living, having turned over the new leaf of life in holy matrimony, fatherhood, motherhood with renewed purpose and Christendom, especially since Heath had made the decision to follow the Lord. Everything would be smooth sailing and Rachel just knew it.

Things were progressing normally from an abnormal past and Rachel began to relax and hope for a better future. She found herself searching more and more for the peace of God. It seemed to be an ongoing impossibility in this spiraling disaster of a past she'd been acquainted with.

Rachel tried hard to hold onto her little unfolding dream, but the heat began to turn up and problems with Mara seemed to surface almost immediately in sharp contrast to the magical knight's tale Rachel had hoped to have with Heath. Though they'd changed both girls names to Billings, along with Rachel's, Mara felt like an outsider now and was confused about her status in this new equation called Mama and new Daddy. Rachel missed the message somehow and even if she'd picked up on it from time to time, Mara was so angry that Rachel couldn't seem to reach her or understand her deep issues. Rachel didn't know how to begin, though she listened for hours as Mara told her her problems, fears and angers. Rachel also made sure Mara went into counseling after the telling of the rape and had made sure she stayed with it, but after Rachel's marriage, Mara began to flatly refuse to go.

Rachel went to her pastor for advice but after several meetings was told that Mara would not survive to reach the age of 16. He said that she would either commit suicide or be murdered because of the rebellious life she was living at the tender age of thirteen. Rachel respected the pastor but flatly disagreed with his interpretation of Mara's future.

"You are wrong!" Rachel cried with conviction. "She will not die! She will live to proclaim the goodness of God!"

The look on his face was one of stunned disbelief but Rachel knew in her heart that the God she knew would not throw them to the wolves this way. Not when they were actively trusting Him to do a miracle. Rachel went home to pray.

She prayed and cried and pleaded and listened and in the stillness of the quiet voice of God, she heard, "I am Mara's Father and will lead her, on her knees, into My kingdom and into her own heart." He said that Rachel was to trust Him, that He loved her even more than she did and Rachel wrote down what He had said, proceeding to try to walk in peace with whatever the future might hold. Every day that Mara lived, Rachel thanked God for another one.

Jenny seemed to get lost in the fallout from time to time and Rachel began to focus on her a little more. She enrolled her in dance classes hoping it would build self-esteem and create a healthy diversion from bad memories. Rachel then got both of them involved in cheer leading and community projects. They attended church. They played putt-putt. They went skating and Rachel bought them everything she and Heath could afford. They gave Mara freedom, they took it away. Rachel danced and danced and danced, but the music never was to Mara's liking and therefore unsuitable for Jenny as well. With every failure, Rachel turned to her heavenly Father in prayer and hope and each new day would bring a new blessing and build a little more faith in Rachel's broken soul.

It was in this plethora of confusion, Rachel again

consulted with her pastor and was led to a support group which met once a week in place of the evening service. There, Rachel met Jerri. Jerri was the leader of the support group and Rachel connected with her in a way she couldn't describe after only one meeting. Jerri knew things about Rachel that even Rachel didn't realize. Things that were clearly outlined simply by following the guidelines of cause and effect in the mysterious world of fear, dysfunctional behavior and emotional disturbances that cripple many, wound some and turn others inward on a quest of learning, knowing, researching every possibility toward healthy emotional response and connection.

CHAPTER 7
THE FAMILY WAY

Heath had wanted very much to have a child of his own and he had asked so nicely Rachel thought now might be a good time, before she got too old to take care of another child. She was already 31 years old. Rachel had made a decision not to have any more children after Jenny but being caught in the flood of desire in Heath's eyes as he'd asked, Rachel had known then with overwhelming conviction that the resounding, "yes....," was the only reply she could make. Rachel now thought a baby to love and care for would bring new life into their befuddled existence as a family. With the first sign of summer amidst the choir of chirping birds and creaking frogs. She got pregnant and with the excitement of a new baby, maintained a semblance of together family life. Mara and Jennifer seemed genuinely happy about the news. When little Hannah Jane was born, they all loved her with a special kind of love. Things seemed to glide for a time with the graceful rhythm of a waltz, except Mara found that along with puberty had come a sense of restlessness and self-defeating behavior that she could not understand, and she ran. She ran to cigarettes, and she ran to boys. She sneaked large amounts of food and alcohol. She ran from Sunday school and wanted more things. She ran from discipline and started slipping out at night to hang out with her "friends". Her "friends" turned out to be gang members and drug users. When Rachel pulled in the reigns, Mara snatched them out of her hands and ran again. Mara had even tried to jump out of the car on the way to a counseling session. Rachel took her to the police station hoping they could help show Mara what happens to minors who don't obey their parents. But the officer just advised Rachel to take a belt to her. Rachel had already tried that and with Mara being a strong girl, it hadn't worked, and Rachel felt, sadly, that she and Heath were at the end of their influence with Mara. Very shortly after, she ran to a boy a little older than she, who wanted to take her to Kentucky. By the time Heath found her the next day, Rachel was in such a panic, not knowing what she might be into and seeing pictures in her mind of her lying face up in a ditch with her throat cut. So, they made the decision to take her straight to an adolescent unit in Birmingham, where she stayed for 14 days without any outside communication for the first seven days.

The letters Rachel got from 13-year-old Mara broke her heart. Mara thought Rachel didn't want her, that Rachel was having a good time without her. That Rachel would leave her there indefinitely. Rachel had told Mara she loved her, needed her, just wanted to help her, but it didn't make a dent. Rachel seemed not to have what Mara needed and it crushed her to believe that. Rachel's limited understanding of parenting skills were becoming evident though she didn't want to admit it. She tried to lean on God, but He seemed to so far away.

Heath and Rachel took Jenny and Hannah to Brianna, and they went to visit Mara as soon as the doctor would let them. In the waiting area of the hospital, they were joined by Mara's doctor and two other men. The doctor spoke about her lack of progress. Mara's future looked dim at best. She had been diagnosed manic depressive and suicidal. Rachel's heart was wrenched in an invisible vise that threatened to cut off her breathing as they sat listening to the doom and gloom of the physician in charge of Mara's case. An awesome black cloud seemed ever near, just above noise level in a timeless vacuum of bad, terrible and worse. Answers seemed to be just out of reach and even impossible to come by. Mara's hope seemed to be in a paralyzed state of maybe, but probably not. This time, Rachel thought, she'll come out of it. She'll respond to truth and maternal love. She'll open up. Rachel vowed to find a way to give her life, if she could just get close enough to reach out and take it.

"I don't know if we can help your daughter, Mr. and Mrs... Billings." The doctor sympathetically declared. "She has a deep rooted shame-base and she does not admit it. She is fighting for survival and she is a master at hiding. We can't seem to get through to her. We don't know if anyone could. The damage done to your daughter happened at such a vulnerable age, she may never recover and may not survive. I'll continue to work with her for another week and then we'll have to release her for insurance purposes. You'll have seven days left on your coverage. The reason for doing it this way is that you will more than likely need us. An attempted suicide or if she decides she wants to cooperate and work toward some closure in this battle going on inside her would be easier for you if you have a few days on your insurance coverage left. She has not allowed our entrance into her trust cathedral at this point, at all. If indeed, she has one. She sees only that her mother is her ticket to wherever she tries to go. My suggestion is, continue her in counseling and hope that she eventually opens up."

After all the necessary questions were answered and they went back through the entire molestation story. Her guts were once again tied in knots from just the trauma of reliving and he stated very dispassionately, "I'm going to let you see her now. Try not to baby her. Be strong, let her know she can't push you around."

Oh, Rachel grew to hate that approach, when all she really wanted to do was take her in her arms and tell her she would do anything it took to see that she had a decent life, a chance, a hope of experiencing the life God intended her to have, full of rainbows and roses, whispers and hugs, beauty and love and the American dream. Rachel couldn't settle for anything less for Mara. Mara was such a huge part of her world and Mara had to live. Rachel willed her to live.

When Rachel saw her, she didn't know what she expected but all she saw was fear. The kind of fear you can't explain. Mara's face seemed flushed with excitement but she maintained her rigid composure as she nonchalantly greeted Rachel and Heath, and the fear was replaced by anger (carefully suppressed and barely evident) and would shift periodically to calculated repose. She seemed to look at Rachel with compassion and a knowledge beyond human comprehension as if to say, "Oh, Mama, why don't you just quit fighting me. You know I'm gonna win and you look so tired. Just give up and let me go." Rachel had seen that look a million times before but never was it so obvious as it seemed at this meeting.

They sat in the cafeteria and had cokes. Rachel asked her what her days were like and she told her she loved her. The tears threatened to come, but Rachel willed them back. Heath, sensing her pain, gave her a brief compassionate glance and his quiet resolve returned as he looked intently into their faces while they tried to make sense of this meeting, this place, this insanity that threatened them both.

"Why didn't you write me, Mama?" She said with sincere surprise.

"They wouldn't let me, Mara. They told me I had to leave you seven days with no communication. I'm sorry, Mara. I've missed you so much, but you have got to let them help you. Honey, we can't handle this alone. Do you like your doctor?" Rachel asked, trying to keep this as light as possible.

"He's an idiot." Mara spat and then softened and added. "Look, Mama, I'm really sorry. Please get me out of here. I'll be good. I promise."

Rachel thought that her heart would break into a million pieces listening to Mara plead to be home with them and Rachel was ill equipped to adequately respond but tried her best to be strong telling Mara that it would just be a little longer. "One more day, honey and we'll take you home." Rachel made Mara promise to be cooperative in counseling. She agreed wholeheartedly. Rachel was hopeful.

As they left, they left hoping that they were doing the right thing and they stayed in Birmingham until the next visitation was allowed and finally, it was time to bring Mara home.

It seemed more than Rachel could bear and when they

went to pick Mara up from the unit Rachel expected everything to be fixed, with a set of answers to put into practice, getting their little girl back all fixed up. Rachel had faith, or so she thought. Mara had convinced Rachel that this had been a miracle shock treatment, that she had seen the light, so to speak. Rachel was guarded but relieved to have Mara close again and as they all piled in the cab of the truck, Mara and Rachel held hands as if they were together again, alone. Just them against everything else. Things were gonna be different, oh, Rachel just knew it. Love had come to stay and they were finally gonna be one, big, happy family. Naturally with her thoughts along this line, Rachel reached over with her left hand and gently took Heath's right bridging the gap between the old and new eras she hoped to join into a semblance of normal good. And still holding Mara's hand with her right, Rachel looked over at Heath giving him a warm tremulous smile. A shared moment, a thank you for helping me help my baby look. Now everything's gonna be all right look. Mara, noticing the exchange, ever so slightly released her hand and when Rachel looked into her face, tears rivered down her tormented flushed cheeks and she looked away as she announced, "I hope you don't think I meant anything I said back there. When I get home, I'm gonna run again." Rachel's rose colored glasses fogged immediately once again.

Unfortunately, Rachel knew Mara's pain to be so great that in that moment she would do exactly as she said she would. That meant running. It seemed that Rachel's first born little girl was so in a state of confusion and despair that no one could reach her, no one. Rachel was beginning to think no one ever could. Her old friend, Devastation, was back and had bested her once more, or so it seemed and her only response to the age-old question came once again in stunned confusion, "Why?"

Mara remained silent and glared out the window of Heath's truck as they went up the ramp leading to the interstate that led home.

Rachel couldn't know then of the vast depth of self-loathing Mara still harbored and of the fears and the uncontrollable anger. Yet every episode of anger-dumping Mara did on Rachel was followed by extreme guilt on her part for hurting the one she loved, her only ally who seemed always there as a stabilizing strength of rescue. But Rachel was not strong enough to break through the encasing of bravado built by the survival experts of Mara's inseparable personalities to protect the little girl locked inside still helpless against her attacker. In years to come, Mara would place herself in situation after situation, similar to the traumatic sexual abuse and domination, like a broken record, replaying the scratch over and over and over until someone strong enough and with a graceful enough hand could pick up the needle arm and begin the music again, beyond the scratch.

Rachel wrote Mara a poem for she couldn't express to her how very much she meant to her.

First Born Girl

I recall the day well when I first felt you stir
In my body, that still cool night
The joy I knew at the life I held
Was warm and full of light

The hope I felt at knowing you
Kept me going day after day
The freedom I sensed at having you
Was like the wind of the ocean spray
It was a beautiful day when the miracle occurred
And I saw you take your first breath
Your precious spirit, even then shown through
And I loved you with new found depth
I held you close and was everything to you
As you were everything to me
The closeness we knew was a miracle
It was warm and good and free
I didn't know love, 'til that moment
I'd never known beauty so rare
'Til I held your little body close to me
Love had never seemed so fair

RACHEL TRIED to share the poem with Mara but she was unaffected and responded with, "Is that supposed to change something?" Rachel felt crushed and powerless, but determined to see Mara through, somehow.

As soon as they arrived home, Rachel began to get nervous and had to stay with Mara the whole night to make sure she didn't sneak out the window. The next morning, Heath suggested taking her with him to visit his mother. While Mara had been gone to Birmingham, Rachel had looked into placing her at the Sheriff's Ranch just in case what happened did, in fact, happen and it looked like the only solution, given the information from Mara's doctor. Though she wanted to believe and hope things could work out right, Rachel felt that her back was against the wall and she had the papers drawn up. Rachel had counseled with every possible counselor about alternatives and she'd prayed every possible prayer. Mara's counselor had written a letter stating that Mara had not responded to counseling and that this appeared to be the most logical next step to ensure her safety. But when Heath's mother found out about the plan, she was very upset. Mrs. Billings begged Rachel to give her a chance and keep her with family. After Rachel had a lengthy conversation with her pastor, she conceded. He'd seemed so smart and even though he appeared to have no compassion, Rachel knew he really cared and was advising her the best he knew how. Rachel was very hopeful that this would work. In all honesty, she couldn't say whether it would have been better this way or better to stay with the original plan of the Sheriff's Ranch. She would continue to wonder about that for quite some time. There were some things you just couldn't know. Mrs. Billings had raised her sister's children when they had gone through a stage of rebellion and acting out behavior and it looked like a safe solution at the time, since Rachel was still working full time and couldn't afford to quit.

Mara started eighth grade at Kinston High and Mrs. Billings treated her like royalty. She bought her a whole new wardrobe and gave her her own room. Mara was allowed to listen to any kind of music she wanted and was even allowed to smoke. Mrs. Billings bought the cigarettes for her. Rachel had always been very strict about her smoking and did not approve this way of doing things. She was all of thirteen and allowed to smoke. Rachel disagreed, but felt her hands were somewhat tied due to the stated commitment previously agreed upon. Smoking wasn't the unforgivable sin and even the pastor had said not to be overly concerned about it.

Mara's new grandparents didn't let her out of their sight and since they lived about seven or eight miles from the nearest town, in the middle of about 20 acres of farm land, Rachel felt fairly good about her safety and she visited as often as she could.

Their first visit was about two weeks after leaving her there and Rachel knew she'd never forget leaving. They both cried almost uncontrollably and the pain Rachel experienced at that separation was a physical vice-grip around her heart and Mara's as well.

Surprisingly Mara seemed to be strangely coming around in this new environment with Heath's parents. Rachel felt at times that her love for Mara was codependent and unhealthy for Mara, that someone else could do a better job at raising her. But then something would happen and Rachel would know Mara needed her more than vice versa. And Rachel would once again pray for strength to be the mother of her wounded little girl who'd had her light put out by the evil of one and needed help to find a way to re-light that candle.

CHAPTER 8

THE HOPE

The relationship between Rachel and Mara became more relaxed in the neutral environment of Heath's mother and Rachel was forced to trust her with her broken little sunflower. Although Mara was only a child, she seemed to have the mind and cravings of a grown woman. Rachel and Mara began to form a different kind of relationship that shifted from a controlling parent, rebelling child to a sisterly admiration and they both took advantage of it, so hungry for acceptance for different, yet similar reasons.

Mara stayed with Mrs. Billings for about one year, give or take and Heath and Rachel continued to work in Montgomery. But they began to have financial challenges. Work was not plentiful enough forcing Heath to work out of town some and to be out of work some which made things worse. Rachel owned the little wooden house behind the coliseum. Well, she and the bank and her daddy owned it, so that was some security.

Jenny bloomed almost overnight, and Hannah went through toddler hood with a lot of health challenges like allergies and asthma. Still, Rachel started to feel like a normal mother with Heath's love and patience being so healing and warm. It was a nice change from their prior lifestyle. When Rachel heard that Mara had been told by Mrs. Billings that Rachel didn't love her or she would have come back for her by now, Rachel knew that Mara needed her mother, or they would run the risk of Mara believing Rachel didn't love her. Which was as far from the truth as it could be. Rachel had never loved anything or anyone more than Mara in her entire life. Rachel began to realize that all her inadequate feelings of mothering Mara were ridiculous and that her own mother was the one thing Mara did need more than anything or anyone else outside of God to feel secure and stable. Or so she thought. Rachel thought she might be shirking her responsibilities as a mother and began to plan to get Mara home with her and Heath so Mara, too, could experience the healing love Heath had been providing the other Billings girls.

Heath was ready to move closer to his family thinking the work would be better and Rachel was getting more and more homesick for Mara as much as Mara was for her. Mara's fears of further victimization from an elderly man who happened to be living somewhat close to Mrs. Billings was voiced in one of her letters to Rachel. It was beginning to look to Rachel as if Mara was about to run again and Rachel's maternal instinct was to protect. Mrs. Billings was getting more and more unwilling to let Mara have the normal relationship Rachel desired and felt they both needed. It became obvious that Mrs. Billings <u>had</u> told Mara that Rachel didn't care about her or she wouldn't have left her in their care for so long. It wasn't long after that revelation that Heath and Rachel decided to move closer to his family for business reasons and Mara for hopefully diverting a disastrous situation. It had begun to appear that Mrs. Billings wouldn't be able to handle Mara after all. Several incidents had come up and Mrs. Billings was obviously putting Mara in a bad light when it was very likely that she was about to become victimized and blamed again at the hands of a close relative. Rachel couldn't take the chance of that being the case and began the plan to get Mara back home with her.

After Heath and Rachel moved to Kinston, they invited Mara over for the weekend that same day, eager to catch up on lost time and give Rachel the chance to look her in the eye as she relayed the events that were a concern. Mrs. Billings refused to let Mara go, however, so after a nice talk with Mrs. Billings, Mara went home with her parents. On the surface, it appeared to be an amicable and appreciative parting. Rachel would never know if it was a mistake or not, but Rachel believed Mara was telling the truth about what she'd heard her new relative say to her and it was definitely inappropriate. There would be no way to know for sure and Rachel never discussed it again with Mrs. Billings believing she'd never believe it of him.

Heath taught Mara how to drive and she seemed to be flourishing in her back home status. They all got involved in church and Mara fell for a guy there that didn't fall for her but made a big ministerial contribution to the "friendship". He was very active in church and would take Mara to youth meetings. She even sang a solo in a church service one night with him in attendance with her. Rachel had heard it was very good and that she had a beautiful voice. Rachel already knew she had a beautiful voice and a beautiful soul. When Mara realized however, that there was never going to be the kind of relationship she desired, it soured her further church going relationship. Rachel tried to keep her motivated but was unable to. Soon it was apparent that Mara had become friends with some wilder kids at school, one of which was the cousin of the boy she'd been infatuated with from church. She began to bring home one undesirable after another until Rachel was fearing the worst, which turned out to be true. Rachel caught Mara sneaking out with the group Rachel disapproved of. Trying to keep her head, Rachel reprimanded and lectured Mara on making the same mistakes. She tried to explain about the dangers of getting involved in the wrong crowd. Mara listened with her ears but her mind pointed her in the wrong direction.

One night, after sneaking out, Mara had stepped out for a smoke on the back patio and upon reentering the house, forgot to lock the back door before turning in for the night. She'd been out earlier that night with a group of obvious miscreants, unbeknownst to Heath and Rachel.

Heath and Rachel had long been asleep and Mara back home when the group of teenagers Mara had partied with earlier had gathered somewhere close to Mara's house for mischief. They had gotten one of their unfortunates drugged up to the point of total obliteration and dropped him off at Mara's telling him it was his house. He evidently believed himself to be home and mistakenly entered the house where Heath and Rachel were still sound asleep, as well as Mara by this time and he proceeded up the hall to the rest room where he partially undressed and relieved himself of a terrible stomach disturbance mostly missing the toilet and accidentally smearing excrement all over the toilet bowl, floor, lavatory, faucet and himself before completely disrobing and climbing into what he thought was his bed, poor sot. The bed, however, was Heath and Rachel's and they had no knowledge of the earlier ongoing events.

Rachel was awakened by a strange smell. She had a nose like a bloodhound. Heath had always teased her about it and evidently it was paying off this time. She smelled something very vile and it woke her up. Looking around she saw nothing unusual but heard something in the hall. As she looked up to the open doorway she saw a man standing in the entrance. Just standing as if he were getting his night vision to see where he was heading. Upon closer observation, Rachel saw that he was naked. Naked! And he began climbing into bed with them. Rachel screamed in earnest and began clawing a path underneath Heath. As she gasped and tried to shake Heath awake she continued to claw all the way to the wall to get away from the naked man and thereby waking Heath up with a start.

"Heath!" Rachel squealed hysterically. "There's a naked man in our bed!"

Heath, seeing her reason for panic and in his befuddled state of a sound sleep, quickly threw the sheet over the stranger's naked body. Heath and Rachel raced out of the room and down the hall in a breathless panic.

When they reached the kitchen, they both looked at each other in horror. Heath, regaining some form of his wits whispered, "Oh my gosh! Get me something!"

Rachel was baffled as to what he wanted her to get him. *He always wants coffee first thing in the morning but.... Get him something? What? Did he want a cup of coffee right now?* She couldn't think... "What?" she asked stupidly.

"Something to hit him with!" He cried emphatically, his face etching alarm and urgency.

"Something to hit him with?" Rachel shrieked in shock. "I'm calling 911..."

"Good idea!" Heath conceded. "Yeah, call 911, but I still need something to hit him with."

"Hit him with? Heath he ain't movin!", Rachel choked out as she frantically grabbed the telephone.

Well, the small town of Kinston they lived in had their dispatch in the next biggest city, Opp, so when Rachel got the 911 operator and explained the situation she was referred to the local sheriff at his home number and told she would have to call him.

"Oh, no..." Rachel groaned. "Not Barney."

Andy Griffith's sidekick in the Mayberry Sheriff's Department, Barney Fife is what they called the local sheriff of Kinston due to his remarkable resemblance and manner.

Rachel called and explained and he said he'd be right there. In the meantime Mara and Jenny had woke up and were standing in their doorway wrapped in blankets with questioning looks on their faces and since their bedroom door faced Heath and Rachel's, Rachel shooed them back into their bedroom and locked the door behind her while Heath waited for the sheriff to oust the smelly intruder.

It was all very frightening for Rachel and Heath. They didn't know if they were about to be murdered in their beds or what, though he didn't appear very aggressive lying there snoring.

Barney arrived in a reasonable amount of time and after assessing the situation by turning on the bedroom light, waking and questioning the sleepy intruder. It was plain that he'd been set up by his "friends" and thought himself to be in his own bed. Barney then had the nerve to ask Rachel if the naked man could shower in their bathroom.

"What?", she replied outraged. "Absolutely not!"

"Wull, I can't handle something like that!", he answered indignantly.

"Take him outside and hose him off," Rachel demanded. "I want him out of my house and he is not showering in our bathroom!"

Barney complied and then requested a pair of shorts to put on him. *"This is unbelievable,"* Rachel thought and rummaged through some of Mara's old clothes trying to find a pair of shorts for this besotted creep who'd scared ten years off her life.

"Here," she offered angrily and she handed Barney the only pair of shorts she could find. *"At least they were Walmart brand instead of Dillard's Sportswear $35.00 Umbros."*

It was on the heels of this time that Mara met an older boy. His name was Travis Wilson and he lived up the street from Mara. She began seeing him on a regular basis and he seemed quite taken with her. He seemed nice to Rachel and Mara seemed inseparable from him. He didn't cuss, didn't smoke. He looked clean cut.

Mara was almost fifteen at the time and Rachel figured it was maybe okay to have a steady boyfriend, especially since he appeared to be a good step up from the seedy characters she'd been hanging with of late. Neither Heath nor Rachel discouraged the relationship too much, though they watched it very closely.

Rachel was coming into a new level of her relationship with God at this time. Heath's role in the family business had become difficult for him to deal with and he felt they needed to move to the next biggest city about 80 miles away to start their own business. This appeared to be a blessing from God for them both. Until they told Mara of their plan.

By this time, Mara had already made her decision that this guy was the one she was going to marry and she refused to move with Rachel and Heath. Rachel couldn't have realized at the time that Mara was acting out in desperate need of love in the only way she felt comfortable with: sexuality. After all her only real experience with male and female issues had been in the framework of perpetrator and victim. This evidently carried over in a sub conscience way that neither of them could see. In her mind someone wanted her and she had felt that could not possibly really happen to her. She was damaged goods. Couldn't relate in the non-victim mentality that her peers did. Her rape had been carefully devised in a caricature of promises and lies. One of which was that Mara was Daniel's girlfriend (though it didn't spare her from his brutish manner or in showing her the knife he kept between his mattresses to ensure her silence) and even later going further into Mara's tortured mind with threats of doing the same to Mara's sister, Jenny, five years younger. Mara had been only six when it started. That would have made Jenny only two years old. Since Rachel had no way of reading the future or Mara's mind, all of these speculations were hidden then from them both.

When Rachel found a house in Dothan, Mara announced that she and Travis were getting married. And if Rachel didn't give her consent, then she would be forced to sneak out and do it anyway, in Tennessee, where it was legal. So Rachel, not wanting to further alienate the relationship between Mara and herself, allowed a small wedding. It was then that Rachel's true education on behavioral habits of the evolving life of a sexual abuse victim began in a spiraling landslide of devastation over and over and over.

CHAPTER 9
THE SET UP

Sometimes, when it's difficult to see clearly what your enemy is up to, it's very possible to get set up repeatedly to recreate the traumas of the past if they're not dealt with properly. That's very likely what took place when Mara had met Travis.

They'd only been married two nights when Rachel noticed bruises on Mara's arms and legs. Rachel questioned her and she said he was pretty rough and laughed it off. The next two years were filled with one rough time after another and from time to time Mara would leave him and come home with little more than the clothes on her back, licking her wounds and keeping most of the relationship to herself. Rachel tried to talk to her but Mara was determined to work it out on her own and Rachel was forced to step aside not knowing how to help or what to do. Every time Mara would come home, Travis would beg her and harass her until she came back. He would call constantly, apologize profusely, charm and finagle until she gave in out of sheer exhaustion and fear that she was a burden on her mothers new family and household.

Usually, her things would come up missing in her absence and that caused more fighting. She miscarried twice during this time due to Travis' lack of desire for an offspring and his violent manner. Rachel felt her involvement in Mara's predicaments led to more problems and she was forced to give up on trying to be a positive influence in Mara's life. When Mara moved the next time she didn't tell Rachel where she lived. She got pregnant a third time and when Rachel questioned her about the relationship and the unstable living arrangements, Mara lied. She told Rachel she had a really nice trailer when really she had been sleeping in a car in a church parking lot for at least one or two months. When Rachel found out, she panicked and did what she had to do to get Mara home. Travis continued to manipulate her into coming back to him and each time there was more abuse and fighting. It was a miracle Mara remained pregnant. Travis was an abusive manipulator and a jobless race car driver in the local racing community where he'd lived most of his life with his three brothers, two sisters, mother and father. His mother carried the financial load in the family by cutting hair and the father was on permanent disability from getting hit by a car and suffering a broken back. Travis appeared to be looking for a similar relationship in Mara. She was the only one with a job most of the time.

When Mara was about four and a half months pregnant and fearing for the welfare of her unborn child, she went home to Rachel and Heath for guidance placing herself totally under their supervision. Of course, Rachel's advice was to go to church and get her life straight, plan a healthy environment for the baby by living at home and divorcing

Travis. It was during this time that Travis agreed to go to church with Mara and get his life straight, too. He and Rachel had several heart to heart talks over the telephone and strict guidelines on staying apart for a substantial amount of time until they could work out his problem with violence. He agreed to every suggestion.

Rachel had bought new clothes for Mara to compliment her growing shape and she was especially pretty one night as prepared to go to church with the family. She wore a pantsuit of tan plaid rayon that seemed to billow around her like a cloud and it gave her a definitive maternal glow of innocent beauty. Travis, however, had planned to attend church with them also and acted like a horny devil all through the church service by leaning too close to Mara and rubbing up next to her, all but fondling her in public. It was most embarrassing and many tongues wagged for weeks about the improper manner of the young estranged husband of Mara Thane Billings Wilson.

Mara's new glowing appearance must have been more than Travis could handle. At the end of the evening, Travis tricked Mara into getting something from the back seat and with her head down and her feet sticking out the window, took off down the dark road at a faster than usual pace.

Rachel knew instinctively when she heard the car speed off that Travis had kidnapped Mara. Running outside to verify her fears, Rachel screamed as she saw Mara's feet thrashing wildly out the window and the car disappearing from sight at a blinding speed. Whirling around and flying back inside the house, Rachel ran into Heath and clutching him around the waist shrieked hysterically, "Travis has taken Mara!"

Heath didn't waste a moment but flew to his car yelling

over his shoulder to call the police. Rachel did that and within a matter of minutes had received word that Mara had been sighted, stopped and was on her way home.

Ten minutes went by and then 20 and Rachel knew something had gone wrong. She called the pastor to pray for Mara and shortly the pastor and his wife arrived at Rachel's door. Rachel was walking the floor and praying with conviction and faith, with a strength not known to her on a natural level but was in fact, supernatural. Soon the pastor and his wife left seeming at a loss for how to console. Needing consolation was the last thing Rachel would allow at that point for her faith was set on Fly, letting nothing catch it but positive strength for more faith. Within a matter of two and a half hours, Heath came driving up in the yard and Mara was with him. Rachel took one look at Mara's torn blouse and the way she held her arm across her chest and knew that there'd been a struggle. Rachel looked instantly to Heath for signs of assault and saw that one ear seemed to be slightly protruding. After hugs, Rachel sat quietly while Mara and Heath relayed the events that had transpired in the two hours giving a surety of a Supernatural Presence with them both.

It seems Heath had trailed them from the time they were supposedly headed back home after being apprehended by the police. At that point Travis had convinced Mara, he would take her directly home not knowing he was being followed by Heath. When Travis encountered Mara's trust factor, he raced off with her to his turf, 60 miles away from Rachel's home, the crux of Travis' threat to his control over Mara.

Upon the arrival of Travis' speeding car into the driveway of his father's home, he had sprung from behind the wheel toward Mara as she had exited the vehicle, running toward Heath. He had pulled up to the curb, stopped the car and with the motor still running waited for Mara. Travis, seeing Mara's flight toward Heath closed the gap between them and grabbed her around the waist trying unsuccessfully to completely stop her progress. Heath, seeing her distress jumped out of his car and ran to aid Mara in her attempt to escape Travis' hold. Heath tackled Travis just as they'd reached Heath's car and had Travis down trying to pris his hands from Mara's belly which he'd strategically clamped in an unbreakable hold. Heath almost had her free when Travis began to yell at the top of his voice to his father and brothers for help. As he yelled and held onto Mara, his brothers began filing out of the house in panicked haste with the father trailing behind wearing nothing more than his wife's black boaed robe and the dazed look of sudden anger at this affront to his otherwise restful repose. First to arrive on the scene was the younger yet largest brother, Cade Wilson, standing slightly over six feet and weighing around 200 pounds. He surveyed the scene and yelled, "What are you doing to my brother?"

To which Heath replied, "He needs to let Mara go. He took her against her will from my yard!" Heath never saw the blow to the left side of his head that knocked him unconscious.

Upon coming to, Heath shook his head to clear it of the cobwebs and shielded with his forearms knowing the fight would be certainly lost by him with these odds. His mind worked as Travis kicked at his middle to Mara's horror and she began to scream, "Don't hurt him! You'll kill him! He has epilepsy!"

The condition hadn't affected Heath since his teens,

controlled by medicine but his attackers didn't know that and it slowed the attack somewhat. With the slight curtail, Heath began to get a slight idea to further Mara's plea and he began to look blankly out past his outstretched arm and billowed out hysterically, "I can't see! I can't see!" Of course Mara began to wail, "Oh my God! What have you done? He can't see!"

The large brutish brother, taken aback began to defend his station and instantly tried to calm the climbing hysteria in the group by sympathetically calling out for Mr. Billings to calm down as he gestured with his hands to hold him down. But Mr. Billings was already on his feet upstaging Patty Duke's Helen Keller role complete with outstretched searching arms as he slyly positioned himself between the crowd and the car inching his progress toward the drivers seat.

The crowd grew panicked, not the least of which was Mara, screaming, "Don't let him drive! He can't see!" She wailed and she peered through the glass of the car window, tears streaming down her creamy cheeks. "Oh, Daddy!" she cried. "What have they done to you?"

Heath almost smiled at the ease with which the insane scene worked to his benefit and he cupped his eyes for a private wink at Mara to which she inhaled sharply and gulped a huge amount of fluid almost choking herself. Though surprised she hid it quickly and with Travis still attached to her hip in a helpless grip of 'Please stay', Mara inched her way to the passenger seat perfectly poised for the scheming get-a-way conspiracy to emerge, still crying but with new purpose. Relief and hope.

Heath pulled the gear to Drive in his already running vehicle and released his foot from the brake. They were soon racing down the street with Travis hanging from the passenger door still clutching Mara's middle and shoulder now in a death-grip vise. Anyone peeking out their windows on Travis' block would have seen a strange entourage of a speeding car, one door open with a passenger attached to the driver, for Heath also had a grip on Mara, and a lanky form attached to the passenger being chased by three grown barefoot men and one slightly questionable person bearing resemblance to a man in a woman's black sheer boa adorned house robe.

Heath drove straight to the police station five blocks away with Travis hanging just far enough out the door that Heath couldn't reach him. When Heath stopped the car in the police station parking lot, he gave Travis the choice, "Let her go and get out of my car or Mara and I will drag you in there and file charges."

Travis knew he'd lost this battle and reluctantly released Mara begging her not to leave him. When Heath and Mara drove away, Travis was lying face down on the asphalt of the police station parking lot crying like a baby. Rachel could see God's hand in this rescue and thanked Him quietly but continually as she got an ice pack for Heath's bruised protruding ear.

CONFUSING HOPE

One would think after the heroics of her new Daddy's rescue of her, Mara would've straightened up, seen the light of "real love", realized the need of her growing baby inside her and embraced the new responsibility of motherhood with maturity, making a wise decision of total separation from her abusive husband. She was back with Travis in less than two months.

Rachel tried to detach her heart from this unborn child knowing it might not survive and tried to distance herself from Mara, conceding that she might indeed die as the preacher had predicted years before.

One day when Rachel's sister, Brianna was visiting in Rachel's home, Mara happened to be in Rachel's home due to yet another explosive fight with Travis. Brianna had known the impossible conditions of the relationship between Travis and Mara, but in a spirit of hope, reached out and placed her hand on Mara's slightly protruding belly praying that God would grow this baby into a fine healthy child. Rachel felt the fear seize her already traumatized heart sensing the faith of their agreement in the prayer. She knew without a doubt that Mara's confused and bewildered state of mind would be determined enough to do whatever she must and that she would now indeed give birth, ready or not, with stars in her eye's based on the desire bigger than anything she'd ever known, to have a baby. Rachel could relate, on some level, knowing the deep desire to be loved and unconsciously allowing a baby of her own to fill that void.

When Little Travis was born, Big Travis was racing and didn't come to the hospital until after the birth even though he knew Mara was in labor and about to give birth. Rachel was there with Mara when she labored to bring him into the world. Rachel's heart panicked when he did not cry and panted like a tired puppy for breath. Her heart of compassion was pummeled with sadness as Mara looked hungrily at the picture the nurse had brought her of her newborn son. Little Travis had inhaled the meconium {thick from the baby's stool in the amniotic fluid} or MAS and it stuck to his lungs like toxic glue. He was rushed to the NICU in Montgomery, where he stayed on oxygen and just a prayer away from a respirator for an entire week. Mara bonded with Rachel in that week like never before, seeming to grasp for faith. Anything to hold on to through this tragedy.

Rachel and Brianna bent their knees and asked God to spare the baby's life. Rachel's heart was hopelessly entangled from that moment on.

Mara appeared so lost at not even being able to hold him and Rachel's love for her spurned her on to pray for little Travis' life to be spared though she knew to go home with Jesus would spare him future pain.

Before Travis was born Rachel couldn't see the hope in his living because of what he would have to live through in the abusive relationship Mara and Travis held on to. Their refusal to seek help for it's tumultuous danger continued to cause great anguish for Rachel. What could this baby have to actually hope for when the chaotic, violence Mara and Travis both seemed drawn to was like a moth to a flame.

Rachel tried to be the supportive mother-in-law rather than the controlling grandparent she knew would alienate her reluctant son-in-law. Yet praying for little Travis and knowing the angels massaged his little chest in the intensive care ward had forever bonded Rachel and Little Travis in a way that could never be broken.

Mara seemed so preoccupied with the disintegration of her relationship with Travis that she appeared incapable of functioning in the realm of motherhood. She seemed to have her priorities way off, in Rachel's opinion, and she worried for the frail condition of the baby. Though she tried to stay in the background, Fate would thrust her again and again to the aid of this child who was so defenseless to withstand the uncompleted maternal instinct of his mother, the cruel abuse of his father, that Rachel knew would one day turn from mother to son.

The day Mara and Travis took Little Travis home was one week to the day from when he had been brought there and when the doctors had determined him well enough to go. Rachel had helped Mara and Travis rent a trailer that was only about 10 miles from Rachel's, hoping for a miracle that they would receive their little treasure with joy and that their lives would move to the upswing hinging on the well being of their new addition to the family.

It just didn't seem destined to happen that way. Travis insisted on Mara and the baby riding home from the hospital, in his broken down piece of a car with no air conditioning in the first week of August. The South Alabama heat that day was suffocating and hot, but Rachel, trying hard not to interfere after being turned down on her gracious offer to let baby and mother ride in the comfort of the air conditioned car, was forced to follow them. She tried desperately not to worry about the fragile condition of the baby and prayed for God to protect him. Travis' pride and control were detestable and Rachel couldn't conceive of a heart so selfish and evil as to not allow available comfort for Mara and the baby. Rachel prayed hard to keep from hating Travis, knowing that hate is not from God.

Travis' car made it half way of the two hour drive home and in a billow of smoke, died in mid throttle directly in front of a small country tavern in the middle of nowhere just outside of Troy. Rachel was allowed to go into the seedy bar for water to pour into the overheated and overworked dilapidated radiator. Travis worked under the hood and would not allow Mara to take the baby to the cool car but insisted she stay in the overheated one while he worked feverishly trying to get it fixed. He ended up repairing a hose with duct tape and with water. It finally cranked up and worked again though somewhat sluggishly, even more so than before. It was a slow next 50 miles, but they all made it and Rachel helped Mara get situated before leaving at her insistence knowing Travis was growing tired of her presence in his home. Rachel prayed all the way home for God to protect the baby and Mara.

Life didn't get off to a great start once the Travis Wilson family arrived home. The baby suffered a small amount right off because Travis wanted Mara to coddle to his whims, forcing her to see to his needs first, while the baby cried. The fighting turned to violence when Mara, fearing Travis would kill the baby in his sleep, was forced to sleep with the baby on her chest and a screwdriver under her pillow. His manhandling brought Mara once again to Rachel for help. Travis had been jealous of the baby and before little Stephen (which Rachel secretly called him) was two weeks old, Travis had already locked Mara out of the house with him and Stephen inside. When Mara was able to break the lock on the door and force her way in finally getting back into the trailer, she saw him sitting on the floor in the baby's room. The baby was on the floor covered in vomit.

Mara somehow convinced Travis to allow a visit to Rachel's that night and while visiting, Travis was seen holding the baby's nose together with his hand over his mouth, just to see what would happen. He had admitted his hate of the baby and Mara knew better than to close her eyes very long.

He had been insistent on intercourse two weeks after

Stephen's birth and Mara was showing signs of a utter fatigue. Her eyes were sunken and dark circles half mooned under them. Her beautiful olive skin seemed ashen like a mask on her face. Rachel knew that if she didn't do something fast, one of them, if not both of them were going to end up dead. She began to plan a rescue.

CHAPTER 10

THE RESCUE

Up to that point Rachel had kissed enough butt that Travis and Mara were letting her keep Stephen every day while they worked and Rachel convinced Mara to go along with a plan to get the baby and herself away from him safely. Rachel didn't have much faith in the Human Resource system, knowing that the baby could end up in foster care should she report this dangerous situation. She felt her only recourse was to take matters into her own hands. After consulting Heath, Rachel planned to get Mara and Stephen to Rachel's aunt in Arizona. It was far enough away that Travis wouldn't be able to follow and Mara could heal in the Arizona sunshine. Rachel felt good about the plan and within a short amount of time, only a few days, the plan was set.

Mara seemed to know that that was the only way the baby would survive and told Rachel she would go along with her plan, but on the day they planned to do it, Mara began to get cold feet and wanted to back out. She was afraid that Travis would do something terrible to the entire Billings family for whisking them away under his nose. Rachel brooked no refusal and in anger and for emphasis, cleared the lamp stand between them as she declared in no uncertain terms that either Mara agreed and helped with the plan or Rachel would be forced to report everything to DHR. Rachel convinced Mara that she would fight for custody of Stephen for Travis putting his life in such danger on a regular basis. Mara finally agreed, knowing Rachel would make good on her threat.

That morning, they went to Mara's trailer to get everything that belonged to her and Stephen, leaving the rest for Travis to deal with. After putting all the big things in storage, they began on Rachel's personal things needed for the trip and they left with Jenny, Hannah and their two Pekingese dogs while Heath finalized a few things that afternoon and left planning to meet them in Birmingham some 120 miles north of where they'd lived. With the baby only three weeks old and while Travis was working only five miles away, Mara and Rachel had made a clean getaway and left town in a matter of less than four hours. Once Rachel and Heath met in Birmingham, they all went caravan style west to Rachel's aunt's house in Arizona.

Travis was seen that afternoon at Heath and Rachel's house, circling it like a savage, waving a gun around and staying there all night awaiting their return, according to neighbors. By then the Billings family was in Birmingham and headed northwest. Rachel, Mara, Stephen, Jenny, Hannah and their two Pekingese in their silver gray 1988 Pontiac Bonneville met Heath in his light blue work truck {roofing truck} and after staying the night in a hotel, headed west. They went through Tupelo, Kentucky and then west for three days through beautiful, picturesque mountains, deserts, Texas plains and finally Show-lo, Arizona where they stayed a week. The scenery was beautiful and on the breezes a cedar aroma filled the warm dry air. The town was smaller than they'd anticipated, and Heath had concerns about their ability to prosper there so they went as far as they could on the savings he had brought. The savings got them as far as Pueblo, Colorado and Heath found work with a local roofing company that same day. To save money, they purchased camping gear and found a campsite that was fairly reasonable. The camp site happened to be in the Pueblo desert. At night, when the sun went down, the western sky was simply majestic and appeared to be filled with fire as jack rabbits scurried to and fro searching for shelter to keep warm through the cold windy nights, even though it was August. Rachel had never seen anything so beautiful, and she breathed in the security of being in one of the most beautiful of God's back yards. The camp site was very convenient, and it seemed as if they were only on vacation in the majestic Rocky Mountains.

 Rachel kept camp and Mara tried to find work feeling that she needed to contribute financially to the cause. Mara's choice of jobs was a saloon type restaurant in the next town, named the Lone Star Bar and Grill. Rachel wasn't really sold on the idea of Mara working in a bar, but she felt that Mara needed it as an outlet. Mara's depression was very obvious and Rachel agreed to care for Stephen. She had tried to give total responsibility of the baby to Mara but the maternal instinct didn't seem to be connecting correctly. Rachel and Stephen bonded even more.

The days were breezy but brutal and the sun could tan you out there in as little as thirty minutes in the afternoon. They'd bought a tarp type covering to shield them from the sweltering desert sun but around 3:00 every afternoon, the wind would blow to such a degree that the canopy would be down on the ground by 4:00 and their grilled hamburgers full of sand so they usually stayed in the tents during that time. Occasionally they would go inside the camp house office and watch T.V. The nights however, were equally as brutal but to the opposite and it would be near freezing, so they had to buy a kerosene heater to heat the tent but it still didn't keep it warm enough. The strange insects that found their way into the tent created more than a few apprehensions, also.

Heath didn't like the people he was having to work with and while Rachel tried to find a house or an apartment that they could get settled in, it became apparent that they were not going to find anything in the area so they stayed only a short time. Heath had called around and located a friend who needed a supervisor in North Carolina. They looked for a place to rent but couldn't find a decent place for less than 1500.00 to 2000.00 dollars down along with a rental reference which they didn't have, so they continued to camp. Tanglewood Campground was a beautiful place with horses and a nice golf course where Arnold Palmer actually held some kind of tournament while the Billings were in residence. Heath and Mara worked and Rachel kept camp.

Mara had found work the first day at a Sub-Shop in town and everyday Rachel would care for Stephen first and then get breakfast for everyone else as they stirred and got hungry. The food had to be kept in plastic storage boxes and bought about every other day due to lack of refrigeration. The dishes were washed under an outdoor spigot. The food had to be put away before bedtime or the raccoons would get into it and ruin everything, which happened several times, before they were forced to buy plastic storage boxes for the food.

The days were peaceful and pleasant and the rustic living had a healing effect on the entire family. Around two months after their arrival, it began to rain and it didn't appear to be stopping. Though they'd fashioned a tarp between the trees to provide shelter, the water began to rise and they had to break camp and go to a hotel for a few nights. The weather turned into tornadoes of devastating proportion throughout the area, reaching all the way to south Alabama where they'd lived and left as a result of Mara's predicament. Camping became impossible because of the weather changes and they were forced to get a loan and buy a used motor home. They found a decent one and slept like babies for the first time since the camping began in their motor home and felt they had survived the elements pretty well. The Winnebago was comfortable and convenient. The Billings family was moving up. It was funny how fighting the elements together could make so many other issues seem so insignificant.

They remained in the camp grounds until it became apparent that financially they were going under due to the shift in the amount of work the owner of company Heath was working for could get and the higher cost of the camp site with the Winnebago. The school year was about to begin and the children needed to get settled in school. They looked and looked for living quarters but were unable to find anything suitable that they could afford, so after they had been gone for about three months, with Mara seeming to have come to her senses and comfortable with the word divorce where Travis was concerned, they went home, to Alabama. The cotton fields were white and Rachel had never been so glad to see them. She hid her tears of sweet pain and joy at going home.

CHAPTER II
GETTING ON WITH THE NOW

Things went well and the Billings returned to their old neighborhood with a minimal amount of gossip coming back to haunt them. They returned to their church and their friends with baby and mama doing well. Mara had plans to get her education and begin responsible living.

Mara had completed her GED training and had passed her test. She began looking for work and trying to expand her horizons. One of the teachers at the Adult Training Center had taken her under her wing and was guiding her to a promising career in office assistant training.

Unfortunately, Mara's interest toward caring for her son had not heightened and Rachel became more and more concerned and more and more bonded with Stephen. Mara seemed unable to connect effectively in meeting the needs of her baby and seemed to see only her own unhappiness. Rachel seemed to hear every night cry and Mara did not.

During this time, the Attorney General's Office found the Billings family and informed Rachel that Daniel had come up for parole. Amanda Bates, the Victim Service Officer, was inquisitive as to whether Rachel was interested in protesting or not and Rachel's knees went weak with fear and dread at the prospect of dragging up again. Would they really be able to?

In addition to the normal proceedings, Daniel's aunt had had her pastor visit with Daniel and try to help with his release by stating that Daniel had told him Rachel had made the whole sexual abuse thing up just out of spite for his mother having married Henry. Rachel was simply jealous. Poor Daniel now had to suffer for a woman scorned, vicious temper and vengeance. That was how Amanda Bates presented it to Rachel.

Rachel digested all of this and thought, "How cruel life could be that just when you had things going in the right direction, something came along to make sure you didn't get too far in the right direction, tempting you to curse God and die." She wasn't ready to throw in the towel though. She began to make contact with friends and get letters of reference, at the urging of Amanda Bates, and decided this might be a good time to request prayer from her church. She called her pastor who had given counsel on several occasions concerning situations with Mara at Rachel's request. Rachel called him to request a character letter be written for her to send to the Attorney General's Office. Her fear seemingly an insurmountable obstacle that his sentence might be overturned on a technicality.

"Brother Harris?" Rachel questioned as he answered the telephone.

"Yes," he softly responded.

"Oh, Brother Harris, I need to speak with you about something," Rachel replied. "Have you got a minute?"

"Sure," he answered. "What is it, Rachel?"

"Well, I was wondering if I could get a letter of character from you to take to court with me," and Rachel recapped all the details for Brother Harris as they had transpired.

She was unprepared for the response that she got from him, however, and it would forever change their relationship.

"Rachel?" he began cautiously. "Are you sure this boy did this?", and he proceeded to tell of a man whose life had been destroyed because of the false accusations of his stepdaughter in a similar state of circumstances.

Rachel was numb. She'd been at Brother Harris' house and poured out her heart about this crime and how it had effected Mara. She had talked at length for hours about it and asked advice from he and his wife about how to help Mara, not getting much practical advice she could use now that she thought about it. Still it was a shock to have her pastor believe that she could actually be part of arresting an innocent man on the whim of a child five years of age, even her own child. It was ludicrous and she told him so but gave him no chance to reply and promptly said her good-byes feeling ultimately forsaken by everyone except the system itself. She thanked God it was there to protect them, for there was no one else to do so.

Before the actual parole hearing, there was to be a private meeting in the Attorney General's Office between the pastor of The Baptist Temple in Montgomery, Reverend Wendall Craig, Rachel, Mara and Jenny. Amanda Bates made it sound as if Daniel had a very good chance of getting an acquittal and Rachel panicked, thinking of how sinister Daniel had seemed at the trial, how Mara and Jenny might be affected at his release and the ludicrous injustice of believing the person responsible for ruining her babies' lives and receiving three twenty five year sentences (to be run consecutively adding up to seventy five years) could actually be free in less than six years.

Rachel could think of no one to help her besides Brett Niles. She searched through the telephone book looking for his name until she realized she'd never find it in there because he was located in another town. Feeling stupid, she picked up the receiver and dialed 411 asking for the number. By the time she got his secretary on the phone, her hand was shaking so badly she had to hold the darn thing still with the other one as well.

"This is Brett Niles," his strong self-assured voice came through the receiver and Rachel began to cry as soon as she heard it.

Trying unsuccessfully to hide her frantic voice, Rachel spoke into the phone, "Um, Brett. This is Rachel Billings."

"I know who it is. How are you?" Brett asked in a friendly tone.

"Not good, Brett. I need to talk to you. The A.G. s' Office called me and…and I know you're a defense attorney now and everything, but I don't know who else to help me," and her voice broke as she tried to continue.

"Calm down now and tell me who from the A.G. s' Office called," he said gently restrained.

Amanda Bates," Rachel answered, still sobbing, holding her hysteria to a controlled solid 7 on the Richter scale. "She said some pastor named Wendell Craig has been visiting Daniel since he was first incarcerated, and Daniel claims I made the whole thing up and after this meeting he could get acquitted! Oh, will you come with us, Brett? I don't think I can handle this alone. I'll pay you for your time."

"Acquitted!?", Brett yelled into the phone causing Rachel to jump and almost drop the damn thing.

"Yes, acquitted!"

"When is this meeting and where?," Brett interrupted.

"In a few days at the A.G.s' office and then the parole hearing will be at the Board of Pardons and Paroles. Will you come?", Rachel sobbed.

"Hell, yes, I'll come. What time?", he demanded.

"10:00 am, on Wednesday, in the conference room and Brett, Mara and Jenny have to be there for him to ask questions!"

"I'll be there, Rachel. Don't worry. I'm not going to let anybody hurt your little girls. Be strong for them now, okay?"

"I will, Brett. Thank you so much. I do feel better knowing you'll come. Thank you, "Rachel said sniffing and beginning to get a hold on her emotions.

"Okay, Rachel, hang in there. I'll see you Wednesday at 9:45 out in the foyer.

"I'll be there. Bye. Oh, and Brett?", she called.

"Yeah?"

"Thank you."

"You're welcome, Rachel. Bye, now."

When Wednesday came Rachel was ready and after speaking with Brett briefly in the foyer before the meeting, she was confident that it would go well.

Amanda Bates seemed quite surprised to see Brett there and Rachel thought she appeared a bit nervous when she announced that Mr. Sessions, the Attorney General could not be present due to an unexpected matter coming up.

Rachel knew Mara and Jenny were nervous, but they were both strengthened by Brett's presence and when the meeting started with Wendall Craig on one side of the table and Mara, Rachel, Brett and then Jenny on the other with Amanda at the head. But on Wendall's side, it had the appearance of a deposition and Wendall spoke first.

He stated his affiliation with Daniel and his continued visitation, Daniel's denial of wrongdoing and his accusations about Rachel's vendetta against his mother for marrying her ex-husband as was claimed by Jackie DeVaughn when she spoke with the pastor about Daniel. His allegations that Rachel was a loose woman and a problem drinker to which Rachel handed the pastor several reference letters of character stating the opposite. One from her counselor, the girl's counselors, from Mara, Jenny and even Jackie's present mother-in-law (who was Rachel's ex-mother-in-law). She then proceeded to tell him the truth about her lack of relationship with Daniel's mother Jackie and the ludicrous reasoning behind going to such extremes of this magnitude simply for spite.

He didn't seem convinced and wanted to question Mara and Jenny alone. Rachel didn't like that idea but knowing Brett would not allow them to be harmed she patted him on the shoulder and left the room momentarily.

Rachel sat in the foyer with Heath and Hannah nervously wondering what they were saying and finally Amanda came out and allowed Rachel back in. Once she was seated again, the pastor seemed confused and said, "Daniel didn't feel his trial was fair, that he was not adequately represented or defended."

Brett was not an enormous man but he was of more than average height and breadth. He had had his arms crossed on the table the entire time looking as though he could pounce at any minute. But at that remark he leaned forward never breaking eye contact with the pastor and bit out, "I would have shot down anyone who tried to defend him. He had three different firms! I'd say that was more than adequate representation!"

At that Amanda looked at Jenny and asked if she would like to say anything. Jenny looked at Wendall Craig just as innocent as when she was four years old and asked, "Is there anything you'd like to ask me?"

He looked as if he might cry and answered softly as he slowly shook his head, "No, Honey. You were just a baby."

After the meeting, Rachel thanked Brett for coming and offered him her address so he could send her a bill, but he refused and said with a friendly wink and sincere smile, "You call me again if you need me. And y'all take care."

With a nod and a shake of Heath's hand and after looking at Hannah, Mara and Jenny, he smiled again and turned to walk toward the elevators.

The parole hearing came and went, leaving in its wake, at least three more years of incarceration for Daniel. Rachel knew she'd gotten two more ulcers and Mara began her downhill spiral at that point. No matter what Rachel did to try and stop it, it was unstoppable.

Mara met and married a young man who had as many, if not more issues than she

to work out, but Rachel and Heath, didn't want to alienate their precariously wired, daughter. So, they gave their blessing and were hopeful since he seemed to really love her. After all, what choice did they really have?

The marriage lasted less than three months due to her new spouse's inability to keep a job and Mara's perpetual date with disaster, by trying to best him in an ongoing alcohol drinking contest and her realization that she'd married a person she not only didn't love but within an unusually short time lost all respect for.

Rachel tried to minister to her daughter as she would anyone who was struggling with life issues, challenges and needs. The outcome seemed to only shed an ominous light on the negligent treatment of Mara's son, Stephen. She appeared to give responsibility of care for her son over to this man she'd married, and his care bordered on frustrated negligence as opposed to her simple negligence, such as not watching and not being aware of fundamental needs for cleanliness, warmth and healthy, timely nourishment. Rachel had helped Mara financially with living arrangements by renting a trailer for her next door. She made sure she saw Stephen at least every day and sometimes kept him for weeks at a time. A lot of the time.

Mara became attracted to a married man with five children and an unhappy, if not disintegrating relationship with his wife of 11 years. His name was Jackson Maine. He was a thirty-two year old, obviously troubled man, with the mannerisms of a child. He looked like a butcher but had the persona of a salesman and a con artist. He had thinning hair and if it had been the 1600's and in England, he could have easily passed for Henry the Eighth. With an inquisitive arch to his brow and a lecherous stare, his demeanor appeared to demand notice. When Mara, complete with make up and swishing a full mane of thick caramel colored hair flashed those piercing green eyes into his bewildered soul, his already troubled marriage took a fatal tumble.

Within a brief two months time, Mara was pregnant with his child. Rachel thought now would have been a good time for a nervous breakdown but she couldn't desert Stephen with so many confusing changes coming in his life not the least of which was the insecurity of which man would be in the role of authority now. Rachel tried to reason with Mara to give custody of Stephen to herself and Heath. Mara refused, but did allow Rachel to baby sit a great deal and when she would come to get him, he would be happy to see her until he realized they were leaving together in Jackson's car. Then he would scream and fight until Rachel could hear the screams in her sleep trying to reason that all babies cry when they don't get what they want. Surely this man was not abusive to this helpless baby of 1 and ½ years . No! Stephen just wanted his Granny, that was it, Rachel would convince herself and pray. She would pray for Stephen's safety, pray for Mara's sanity, pray for reprieve from the nightmare she was living. But the prayers seemed to be hitting the ceiling and bouncing back to mock her for all she was worth because Mara moved 150 miles away without so much as a good-bye, snatching Stephen from the only stable environment he'd ever really known.

Mara stayed in semi-contact with Rachel, especially if Mara needed money and with Stephen's two-year-old birthday coming, Rachel and Heath were allowed to come to his party which consisted of Jackson, Mara, Rachel, Heath, Hannah, Jenny and Stephen. Mara had gotten him a nice cake and balloons decorated the small one-bedroom house just off the main street of Tallahassee, Florida. Rachel was on pins and needles the entire night, knowing something was up. Mara was being too nice, too accommodatingly pleasant. No doubt about it, Mara was up to something, but Rachel just couldn't quite get the vision of what it could be.

Stephen brought Rachel from her musings by squealing with delight over his big red truck he had gotten for his birthday and chasing Hannah, now 7 years of sweet fragile love. Hannah was dodging him and ducking behind furniture giving him just enough room to believe he could catch her. Then she would dodge him again. She appeared so out of place in the threadbare little house, as did Mara and Stephen. Why Mara wouldn't allow her family to help her stay financially stable was baffling to Rachel. Truly baffling.

CHAPTER 12
THE TEMPORARY REPRIEVE FOR MARA

Rachel had begun her day with the usual chores and prayers for the family, peace for the world, love for the hurting. Upon completing them she drove to town to run some errands and was just finishing up when the cell phone rang.

"Mama?" Mara called into the receiver when Rachel answered.

"Mara!" Rachel called back and smiled inside, "Hey! How are you?"

"Are you on the road, Mama?" Mara asked with an unusual air to her voice that sounded as if she were in a tunnel. Rachel thought maybe they had a bad connection.

"Yeah, I was running some errands. Are you okay, Mara? You sound funny."

"Oh, yeah, I'm fine, but um you better pull over, I've got some news for you," she said with a controlled exhilaration.

Rachel was, well there was that word again, baffled. She pulled into a Shell station and put her car in Park leaving the air running. It was hot as an oven outside. "Okay," she sighed trying to will her emotional antennae down so she wouldn't over react no matter what it was, for she couldn't quite shake this feeling of a storm brewing. She tried to remain calm. "What is it, Mara?"

"Are you pulled over?" Mara questioned.

"Yes!" Rachel answered impatiently. "Now, what is it?"

"Well, you know I've wanted to see the world and travel. I've decided to move to Alaska."

"Now, Mara," Rachel interrupted with ....

"Mama. I'm at the Canadian Border. I'm on my way to Alaska," and there was dead silence on both ends of the phone.

'Oh, God, there isn't any air in here to breathe.' Even though the air vents were blowing her hair back like the winds from the frozen tundra. Suddenly there was a scream like that of a terrified woman fighting for her life as her attacker was dealing attempted death blows to her head. Rachel heard it, too and looked around her outside the car to see what it was. People were looking at her. 'Oh, God, it couldn't have been me. No, God, no, God.' Her mind screamed and she heard it again.

Rachel was always one to think fast on her feet and squelched down that last scream which threatened to tear her mind apart.

"Put Jackson on the phone," she bit out to Mara.

"Hello," Jackson answered in his smug little, "Gotcha," voice and he giggled his sinister giggle that set Rachel's spiritual talons on edge.

"Jackson?" Rachel said deadly soft and continued in the same quiet tone and Jackson didn't make a sound as he listened knowing he'd gotten all the cookies out of the jar and no one could catch him. But he still had a healthy fear of the unknown, which Rachel definitely was for him. "If anything happens to my daughter and my grandson, there will be no place you can hide from me because I will make it my life's work to have you hunted down. Do you understand me?"

"I swear, Rachel, nothings gonna happen to them," and his manner grew ugly. "Whether you believe it or not, I happen to be in love with your daughter and I only want what's best for her," and with that he handed the phone to Mara.

"Mama, we're gonna be fine," she commented gaily as if she were just going into the next room to watch a program on T.V. and so excited at the prospect of seeing this particular show. "I'll call you when we get there," and with that she hung up. Rachel dropped the phone on the floor as she dropped her head on the steering wheel and cried in earnest. In fear and in shame.

She didn't know how long she'd been there when she looked up but the sky looked cloudy and the sun had moved from the high noon position, telling Rachel it wouldn't be long before Hannah would be getting out of school. She headed home in shock, in a surreal dazed mode that she couldn't quite shake.

On OCTOBER 25, 1997, Rachel went back into therapy. The fear for Stephen's safety was overwhelming. Jenny had begun to show signs of being possibly suicidal and she also had to go into therapy. By the time she turned fifteen, she was becoming the angry, unreasonable child that Mara had once been. It was worse than Deja vu because of the vast difference in the temperaments of the two. Mara had been mild mannered and stubborn where Jenny would be high strung, outspoken and strong willed, along with being stubborn. It was quite a dose and Rachel found it more than she alone could abide.

Rachel got Jenny into therapy and found that she'd been practicing bulimic activity. Rachel had sat in on several sessions at Jenny's request. The counselor they'd found hadn't had a lot of experience with eating disorders but had had some. She was a Christian Counselor, so Rachel and Jenny trusted her.

Jenny seemed to improve somewhat but wasn't fond of counseling. She wanted to be with her friends and feel normal as she perceived everyone else was.

Rachel went to counseling regularly and was encouraged to turn Stephen's care over to God and his mother, reminding Rachel that raising Stephen was not her responsibility. She tried so very hard to do that and by praying every day, trusting God and writing poetry, within a year, she felt somewhat better trying to leave things in the hands of God. She tried to concentrate on Jenny and Hannah, but it's awfully hard to teach a heart not to do everything within its power to love a child you love and that you know isn't getting the full benefit of that love where he is.

Mara seemed to be a different person when she would call Rachel. She would talk about how beautiful everything was there. How she felt that it was a good move. That she could feel all churned up inside and look out at the snow falling so softly and clean and she'd feel clean just being a part of it all. She referred to the fact that too many bad memories were in Alabama to face on a regular basis and

Alaska was wonderful. A new place with a new start and a new life. She'd send a dozen postcards at a time and Rachel became an expert on Alaskan Historical Sites within a few months' time. Mara talked only of Alaska and Rachel began to feel that if she were going to be a part of Mara and Stephen's life from here on out, she'd better learn to like, no to love Alaska, and she did.

Mara mentioned in early October that the baby would be coming around the 10th of November and asked if Rachel could come to help her for a week when the baby did come. At Rachel's hesitation, Mara mentioned the problem Stephen was having with his penis foreskin and how a doctor there had recommended circumcision. Mara thought Rachel could come and take care of helping with that, too. Rachel knew that Stephen would need her and knew she had no choice but to come. Financially and emotionally, it was a stretch. Rachel shoved that into Inconsequential.

Mara spoke of getting work and Rachel panicked wondering where Stephen would be and who would be caring for him, knowing that it would be Jackson. And to Rachel, this man was virtually a stranger. Jackson would be alone with her Stephen at two and half years of age and 4300 miles away. Rachel got on her knees. She began to develop a relationship tighter than she ever knew she could with her Heavenly Father and at times would be at ease with it all. Other times, it was obvious that Stephen was not getting the proper care nor the proper type of discipline when Mara wasn't around to watch him. Yet, Mara trusted Jackson completely and as Stephen was Mara's baby, Rachel was forced to trust him, too.

Rachel had made plans to get a flight on Mara's due date and had made all the necessary arrangements for the trip, but on October 31, 1997, Mara called from the hospital in Alaska and announced that her labor had begun. Rachel tried everything but could not get to Mara without it costing more than any of them had access to. She got the earliest flight available in the price range she had to remain in and was on a plane to Alaska by November 10, 1997.

CHAPTER 13

THE MARTYR

The flight was eleven hours long and tiresome but Rachel utilized the time to reflect on the coming visit and how to get insight from God. She hoped she was gleaning true wisdom on how to conduct herself in the home of Jackson and Mara. After all that had transpired between the three of them, not to mention the fact that Jackson and Mara lived together, unmarried, with Rachel's grandson and the heated vibrations that seemed to be ever-present with every encounter, Rachel had to admit, she was at odds as to how to deal with it all. After several poems and supernatural comfort from the Holy Spirit, when Rachel's feet touched the walkway from the plane at the Alaska airport, she felt ready to face anything. The crowd pressed around her in haste trying to reach their loved ones waiting for them in the airport. Rachel maintained her balance in spite of the push but was totally unprepared for the avalanche of emotions that would rock her heart off its rhythm beat when she saw Mara standing at the end of the walkway, holding Stephen's hand. All Rachel could see was

Stephen's eyes round with anticipation. But knowing that Jackson stood just beyond her holding the baby carrier, she knew she had to share herself, not showing partiality.

Rachel dropped her bags and reached out for Mara as she melted against Rachel's hair wetting it with her tears. Rachel pulled back and looked full into her face as they both laughed, and Rachel's heart tore a little more for her little sunshine girl with the big heart and wide open dreams. She looked down at Stephen who was staring blankly at Rachel as if he couldn't believe it and Mara called down to him, "I told you Granny was coming! It's Granny!" And he catapulted into Rachel's outstretched arms with such force they almost landed on the ground. Rachel picked him up and rocked him and wet his hair with her tears. "Oh, Stephen, Stephen," she cried into his scattered soul. "I missed you, so much. I miss you, so much, Stephen," and he clung to her as though his life was at stake.

After a long, long hug, Rachel put Stephen down, still holding his hand and asking if he'd gotten a baby sister. She got her first look at Monica, all pink and soft in her little carrier and topped with a healthy swatch of dark sable hair. She was asleep. Her little nose and face reminded Rachel instantly of Mara when she was small, and Rachel had to keep a tight rein on her heart for fear she'd lose a bit more of it here.

With a polite greeting and a nod to Jackson, Rachel followed Mara to the baggage claim and as they stood there waiting for the luggage to make its way around the conveyor, Mara turned and looked at Rachel as if she couldn't get enough. And yet her guard was up somehow as if she didn't know what to expect from this visit. She reminded Rachel of a small child who'd been caught in the act of.... something. Something Rachel couldn't put her mental finger on and guessed that neither could Mara. Once they located the bags, Rachel followed Mara out of the airport and into a gush of cold air that took Rachel's breath away. Looking past the line of cars parked at the entrance door, she got her first glimpse of the frozen tundra, as Mara had come to view it. It looked like a Christmas card everywhere. The Blue Spruce trees were surrounded with glistening powdery snow tipping the ends like decorations, all white and perfect. Rachel began to see the reason for the smile in Mara's heart at being in this untouched wilderness, called the Last Frontier.

Jackson sat with the baby in the car while Rachel and Mara loaded the bags into the trunk and Rachel was holding her coat together by the time she got into the car, trying not to slip on the patches of ice splotching the paved roadway where the car was parked. Stephen seemed to glide easily over the ice in his mountain boots.

Jackson pointed out landmarks along the way and told little stories about his childhood, growing up in this magical place. Rachel listened halfheartedly and couldn't see much of the view for staring at Stephen, Monica and Mara.

Once they reached the apartment and everyone got settled in the living room, Rachel sat down, and Stephen promptly walked over to her. He crawled up in her lap as if to say, "I know this person loves me and would never, ever reject me," And he was right.

Jackson viewed this scene with interest and commented, "He doesn't do that with us." Rachel felt the bile rise up in the back of her throat and she knew why she was really here. This man didn't want this child (this child who was so much a part of her) and wanted Rachel to take him home with her.

Now that Jackson's household showed four dependents on paper and he'd get the Alaska dividend worth $1500.00 per child, plus the Aid to Dependent Children he'd helped Mara file as a result of Stephen's daddy not paying child support, he didn't, in Rachel's opinion, care what happened to Stephen. Jackson was a businessman, after all and he'd gotten a rough deal from the woman scorned in his and Mara's affair, so it was likely difficult to love this confused and resentful toddler. Rachel tried to understand.

Jackson's pending ex-wife would have custody of his five children and he would have no visitation rights since she had supposedly staged an elaborate domestic abuse scene in order to get charges filed and when Jackson left for Alaska, they stuck like glue, burning the bridge between Alaska and Alabama for Jackson and now Mara, who had Stephen in their precarious custody.

Jackson talked and Rachel listened, and it became obvious that Jackson was in charge of child-care a good bit of the time while Mara looked for work or worked. In one conversation Jackson shared how Stephen had excreted on the floor in six separate places out of spite because he simply resented Jackson. Stephen's punishment was to stand in a corner, unwashed for an hour. Rachel's blood began to boil, but she tried to appear calm and shared a few helpful hints on child-rearing though she wanted to take both children and running screaming down the street, hitching a ride to the airport and calling Heath to get them home. What was she saying? She wanted to take Mara, too.! This man had all the sensitivity of a Brillo pad and Mara was off in with him, in his Godforsaken cave. *"Get a hold of your-*

self, Rachel," she thoughtfully admonished sternly. *The war can't be won by running from the battle, you must stay and fight this one out, if you want to win at all with Mara.* At least she'd be allowed to take Stephen home with her for a while and he'd be with her through Thanksgiving and Christmas. Maybe, Rachel prayed, Mara would let him stay.

The bond between Stephen and Rachel could not be denied and it was much of the motivating factor for Rachel to keep going. It was like carrying a wounded man on the battlefield. Sure, it was a load, but how else could you get him to safety? Rachel considered getting DHR involved as she had once threatened to Mara, but the thought of Stephen ending up in the system with no promise of his being able to come to her quickly squelched that idea all to pieces and Rachel made up her mind that she would carry Stephen and Mara and now Monica as far as her legs would hold her up.

The four days were uncomfortable for Rachel with the Alaska ice being inconvenient and scary thought she'd never seen a more beautiful place. There was blinding white snow everywhere her eyes touched along the streets and the trees all looked gothic and like Christmas with massive majestic, white mountains dazzling the sky as far as the eye could see. When the wind caught snow dust billowing it around, Rachel was reminded of Frosty the Snowman scenes she had seen on T.V. when she was a little girl. It was a mystical place and appeared surreal. The sun never actually came out but seemed to peek slightly from behind the clouds for only an hour or two a day.

Mara had gone to some trouble to see that accommodations were comfortable for Rachel, but it was awkward none-the-less and Rachel was ambiguously glad when the plane lifted into the dark Alaska sky heading toward Seattle and ultimately home.

The flight was tiring and a bit uncomfortable since Stephen was circumcised the day Rachel had arrived. Rachel held him as he slept the night through and upon waking, they were both wet. Stephen had peed them both, though he rarely had accidents. Obviously, the surgery had affected his judgment and feeling. Rachel wasn't prepared for the accident other than baby wipes and since the bags were checked she was forced to continue the 12-hour flight before arriving home, in semi-damp clothes spread lavishly with cologne.

Dothan, Alabama was looking exceptionally good when Heath drove them through the city and home to their hundred-year-old wood frame house in the country. The tall white plantation-built house stood serenely nestled in the several pecan trees, crate myrtle trees, pear trees and azalea bushes. Though truly little was in bloom on the corner lot surrounded by three acres of wooded greenery and plowed fields on every side but one, at the front corner of the lawn a beautiful winter bush bloomed lavender flowers along the strong umbrella shaped limbs sweeping the ground. It seemed to bring peace to Rachel's jet-lagged, war-worn spirit. A smile crept up from her heart and looking over at Heath, his silent strength unwavering as he drove through the yard to the front door, Rachel breathed in the safety of home.

Thanksgiving came and went, and Christmas was coming fast. Rachel took pictures of Stephen, shot video of him, prayed with, for him and tried to give security to his befuddled little mind. He was beautiful and so happy to be with the family he'd been born into, loved, nurtured, and mostly raised by. Rachel wanted to keep him, but every advice was that he belonged to her daughter and not to her. Rachel began to doubt her own motives in wanting him, convincing herself that she should trust God more and allow his mother to make the decisions for her own son. After all, God had given him to Mara, not Rachel and Rachel didn't want to interfere in what God wanted to do in Mara's life. Rachel went from confusion to a powerful desire to mother and protect Stephen feeling that he wasn't getting what he needed to mature normally. The decision was taken from her in January when Mara arrived almost unannounced more than ready to have her family complete by taking Stephen home with them where she insisted, he belonged. Rachel just knew there was something not quite right, but she didn't feel she had the right to keep him. This gave Rachel no recourse but to give her son to her, though she knew the separation would be hard on Stephen. She tried to explain what was about to take place, but nothing could have prepared either of them for the scene at the airport.

Mara and Jackson's flight was called and with Stephen's left hand in Mara's right and his right hand in Rachel's left, Rachel couldn't speak when she had to let go at the gate but tried to keep her face in a happy, it's going to be okay, mode. Stephen clutched air as he reached for Rachel's hand and looking over his shoulder, he called out urgently, "C'mon, Granny!"

"I can't go, baby," Rachel squeaked out. "Remember? I told you I couldn't come home with you, honey. You have to go home with your Mama." She heard his distressed objection as he suddenly realized what Rachel had been trying to tell him and he had been unwilling to acknowledge. Finally, the noise of the engines drowned out his wailing misery.

Rachel was exhausted but even more than that, she was emotionally drained and had to lean on the Lord more than ever after this separation vowing to keep in close contact with Mara whether Mara liked it or not and Rachel began thinking of ways. Unwittingly she thought moving to Alaska was the thing to do, praying it would end the continual ache in her heart and in her gut. She started praying for clearance from God on that very thing but rather than praying for answers, she prayed merely for help to accomplish her plan. She began forming the relationship stronger with Mara and spoke with her often as possible while scheming internally how to move the family to Alaska, to be near Stephen and see to his wellbeing. She felt peace with her decision and drafted this poem January 28, 1998. Stephen was two and a half years old.

Mercy surrounds me, grace abounds
My own grace to others, is making its rounds
So grateful I am, to know Your Name
And using Its power, has ended my shame
I want Your Presence today and always
Your love and Your peace, my weary soul craves
Thank You for choosing to give me life
And making me free to live without strife.

CHAPTER 14
THE CONVINCING AND THE RELOCATION

As was her usual solution in a tight, she decided everything would be easier if the family was geographically closer. Rachel began pleading with Heath to allow her to make the move to Alaska. A clean start for Jenny might be a good thing and she could keep a close eye on Stephen. Stable Heath was at a loss as to how they were ever going to get ahead financially if Rachel continued to think with her broken heart this way and chase her confused and bitter daughter around the countryside. But after researching the opportunities in Alaska, it looked doable if Rachel got a job and could get them financially stable, find them a place to live and get the children in school. Rachel made several calls, trusted Mara for some strange reason she couldn't quite understand and within a relatively brief time had faxed her resume to Quadco, a large oil company that wanted to hire her at $20.00 per hour. It looked good and Heath agreed.

Rachel began packing up for the move expecting to start their new life in the Last Frontier. Jenny and Hannah were packing with enthusiasm, but Jenny was a little apprehensive about being that close to her troubled sister again, though she never told Rachel about her feelings and Rachel had the illusion of 100% support from every member of the family.

After much preparation, booking flights and buying the necessary items for the climate change, they were off. It was exciting to be going to a new place, a new vision, a new hope. The flight was perfect except for the minor headaches the girls suffered due to the elevation. Rachel provided gum, Tylenol and sympathy throughout the long flight, writing a travel log and poetry.

Arriving at the airport, Rachel called Mara to let her know their flight had arrived in Anchorage and Mara seemed to be in the middle of a disturbance with Jackson. Rachel let Mara know it wasn't a problem, they were catching a cab to the Northern Lights Hotel, and she could call later.

"No, Mama. Call me when you all get settled and I'll come over," Mara insisted timorously.

Rachel hung up the telephone having a sense of something wrong but unable to identify the problem. She began to unpack and get the rooms in order knowing the following day she'd be able to get a car since she'd sent $500.00 to Jackson at his suggestion to secure the vehicle for her. Jenny and Hannah were checking out the rooms when the telephone rang

"Hey, Mama, it's me," Mara said when Rachel answered.

"Mara!," Rachel said excitedly. "Come on up."

"Well, I can't right now, Mama. Jackson's not in a good mood and the kids are in the car. Can you just come out for a minute? We have to run some errands."

"Um, well sure I can. What's wrong?," Rachel asked, concerned about more than just Jackson's fit and feeling the sharp pain of the children's obvious distress in the presence of one of Jackson's fits, not knowing Jackson well enough to know what that would entail.

"Oh, it's nothing, Mama. He's just upset because the car he bought for you is buried in the snow and the man he bought it from says he can't get to it until the ice melts and he can get the other cars blocking it out," Mara said offhandedly but with some trepidation.

"Well, let's not worry about that right now," Rachel assured her. "Let me get my boots on and I'll come out to see the kids."

"Oh, good. I'm glad you're okay with it. We're in the parking lot to the right when you come out the front door."

What Rachel saw broke her wounded heart again. Jackson was behind the wheel of a dirty old car with Stephen and Monica strapped in car seats of an even dirtier back seat. Rachel's indignation at the injustice of child neglect soared. She shoved it all down reminding herself of the goal in mind and smiled sweetly at the children putting her love's foot forward greeting them warmly, excitedly, squelching down the tearful emotion to rescue knowing Jesus to be the only real Rescuer in any and all situations, including children. *What was she saying! Especially children. Jesus loves the little children. Right?*

Mara threw down her cigarette and embraced Rachel passively.

"Granny!" Stephen squealed and tried unsuccessfully to free himself from the horrid straps holding him tightly to the car seat.

"Oh! Baby, I missed you!" Rachel cried as she reached in

and crawled into the car. "Hey, Baby!," she smiled to Monica capturing her inquisitive bright blue eyes and reaching over to caress her soft smudged little cheeks. She pulled slightly away not knowing who was touching her and Rachel felt the anger toward Jackson rise in her heart at taking these babies so far from their family. She held it in check and greeted him politely, to which he grunted a semi-cordial reply leaving no question to his resentment of her presence in "his" town. *What a con he was.*

Mara stood outside the car waiting for the greetings to be over so they could be on their way leaving Rachel with a promise to call on completion of their errands. Rachel wondered at their cool reception but would not allow it to occupy her mind for long. She had bigger problems at present, one being the need of a vehicle. She went back inside the hotel calling for Hannah to follow. After all, it was up to her to see to it they could survive in this new town that resembled an enormous iceberg.

"But I wanna play in the snow, Mama," she pleaded energetically as she kicked sparkling snow dust into the air with her snow boots. Rachel made a mental note to buy a camera first chance she got.

"Okay," Rachel conceded, "but just for a few minutes, we have to get a car so I can get a job. You want to live here, don't you?"

"Oh, yes," Hannah bubbled, "I do," throwing balls of snow in the air and trying to catch them.

Rachel had little conception of how Anchorage ran things and after earnestly speaking to the hotel attendant she realized she'd planned her arrival at the two-week celebration of Iditarod, the huge dog sled race which everyone took their vacation to either view or participate in. And she began to worry that she'd run out of money before making any real headway. After several phone calls to companies interested in hiring her when she'd made contact from Alabama, her fears were realized, and she got the same response from all of them.

"The person in charge of interviews and hiring won't be back in the office until Monday, December 3rd."

Rachel's hopes were dashed but her determination was not, and she made plans for applying anywhere, including the hotel restaurants, but it seemed no one was interested in hiring someone with no address other than Room 213 at the Northern Lights Hotel. After a week had passed, Rachel gathered the kids together, got in their rental car and set out to enjoy Iditarod herself. There were ice sculptures on the shore of the North Atlantic Ocean at the edge of town that were incredible. A polar bear was sculptured in such detail, it was almost eerie. There was a fishing boat complete with fishermen, poles, and fish on the line. There were Eskimo families and igloos, seals, and walruses. There were moose and caribou. There was even a huge replica of the famous naked lady mountain that can be seen from the shoreline, lying peacefully on the water of the North Atlantic Ocean. Everything everywhere was frozen ice or white powdered snow that sparkled in the horizontal aligned sun. Buildings all had white roofed, and snow tipped trees resembling cozy Christmas cards everywhere they looked.

Mara and Jackson had arranged a snow sledding trip for the whole family at a park several miles outside of town and Stephen, along with his sister Monica chattered and played relentlessly in the back seat on the way. Hannah tickled them and joined in their play, excited about the prospect of sledding, also.

The hill Mara and Jackson had chosen was in sight of a small playground and from the top it was evident that Anchorage sits in the middle of a large bowl of sorts with white, majestic mountains, side by side in a complete circle, giving it the appearance of a surreal wonderland in another world.

Rachel watched as the children, already there, boarded their sleds and scooted to the edge, propelling themselves with their hands on either side of the sleds, then pulling them in as gravity took over and the mounted sleds began their downhill slide, causing their scarves to flap wildly behind and squeals of delight to come forth. Hannah boarded her round red sled calling for Rachel to ride with her. Rachel thought about declining but the look in Hannah's large brown eyes were lit up like the Northern Lights. The yearning in her animated smile reminded Rachel of an angel, happy with delight over an unusual gift. She couldn't say no to that face and found herself climbing behind Hannah. They were soon swirling down the snow dusted hill with carefree abandon. But Rachel's heart was far from carefree. She felt as if the life of her child was in her hands and yet, it was not. It was in the hands of her daughter. The daughter who seemed to make one bad decision after another, placing her innocent son in harm's way so often, right down to the pants he wore that were nowhere near thick enough for the frigid cold. The gloves he wore were Rachel's because Mara had lost his and he had no hat on. Rachel felt his cold and tried to talk Mara into letting her go to Walmart to get some warmer clothing for him. She replied in the negative stating that "he got too hot with all that stuff on." He was used to the cold and besides, he'd just lose them anyway. Rachel knew better than to argue with her, but she checked regularly to make sure he wasn't too cold, gave him her gloves and scarf and they didn't stay long.

At the bottom of the hill, she saw a strange shape to the left of her resembling a horse of sorts walking by the trees close to the playground and upon closer speculation realized it was a moose. 'Alaska,' she thought, 'The Last Frontier. What a wonderful place.'

Stephen broke through her thoughts calling, "Come on, Granny!"

Mara was about to ride with Stephen down the hill and he wanted his granny to board the small sled with them. "I'll do it next time, baby," Rachel answered, and they took their ride.

They all took the plunge several times and after Rachel had gotten several pictures, she decided it was time to head in for dinner as she knew the children must be getting hungry by then, and cold as well.

The week passed quickly and still Rachel had not found work. The hotel was too expensive, and Jackson and Mara's house was too small to accommodate Rachel's family of three. Jackson was not able to get the car Rachel needed and he had also been unable to come up with the money that Rachel had paid him. Soon, it became obvious, Rachel would have to return home, without Stephen and it was a trying trip back. Rachel tried to talk to Mara about taking Stephen home with her. She tried to reason with her about what was best for Stephen and that it was fairly obvious that they would have problems concerning him. Mara didn't seem to compute any of Rachel's concerns. All Mara could see was her family, her son and she was not giving him up. She was still holding on to the dream of unreality input and perfected output. It equated to not looking toward the future of which Rachel could already see and Mara could not, nor would she allow Rachel to ruin her dream. Rachel had no choice but to trust God for Stephen's safety and leave her babies in Alaska without her.

CHAPTER 15
THE INSANITY

After several weeks of being back home Mara called Rachel in a panic stating that Jackson was going to take custody of the children. Mara had become upset with his continued inability to hang on to the family income due to a sustaining cocaine habit (which Mara had neglected to tell Rachel about) and they had gotten into a big fight. Mara had tried to leave, and Jackson went to the magistrate to file for custody.

Alaska law being what it was, in a family dispute, the first parent to file was awarded custody of the children if it appeared the other parent might leave the state with them, and it looked like Stephen would be in the potentially dangerous and neglectful grip of his stepfather. Rachel panicked, too, and after several phone calls Rachel had Mara and the children in a shelter for battered women, flown some four hundred miles away to Kenai.

After an appearance before family court, since both parents had brought forth questionable conduct it began to look as though both Jackson and Mara could lose custody altogether due to the accusations. Mara's fear of being without her children even for a little while during investigations spooked her enough to cause her to drop the allegations, as did Jackson and they went home together. Rachel worried, prayed, stayed in close contact with Mara and with Stephen and tried to figure out a way to "fix" the situation, thinking of no other way than taking Stephen out of the equation. It seemed he was the constant topic of conflict between Mara and Jackson. And a constant concern for Rachel.

JENNIFER'S HOPES

Rachel had little time to dwell on what she had no control over and was forced to pay close attention to Jenny's seemingly spiral downward. At age fourteen, Heath had adopted Jenny for her birthday. Rachel had told her that he had wanted to when they first married when Jenny was six years old. But Rachel made it clear that it was her decision and by the time she was 13 ½ she'd made that decision. She had made several attempts to connect with Henry, her biological father, hoping for affirmation of his love for her. He would seem to respond and show interest but when it came to contacting or communicating with her there was just nothing there outside of one letter, one small birthday gift and one phone call in seven years. Though Rachel had never talked against Henry to Jenny or Mara and had never tried to stand in the way of them forming a relationship with him, his distant uncommunicative manner had.

After the adoption, the failed attempt at relocation to

Alaska, back home to the wood frame house in the Dothan area, Jenny began to date. Heath and Rachel tried hard to keep her boundaries regulated with her dating activities and overall Jenny kept in close contact, relatively speaking, with Rachel on important issues. Jenny felt particularly good about herself because she was a virgin when many of her peers had long since lost their virginity.

Jenny was very secretive about her past abuse and only with her best friend of several years and her counselors had she shared it. Unfortunately, this friend was the friend of a girl Jenny didn't know who had an attractive older brother, two and a half years Jenny's senior, who saw Jenny at the movies one night and was stricken dumb with infatuation instantly. His name was Paul Cummings and after meeting Jenny, he aggravated his sister Leah about fixing him up with her. She tried to discourage her brother from possible involvement with her but when he persisted telling her he'd never seen a more beautiful girl and one with such light and innocence, she told him about Jenny's childhood sexual abuse, hoping it would deter his desire for involvement.

From then on, he was on a mission to have Jenny, possibly hearing talk about adult children who'd been molested becoming promiscuous. Jenny was not the status quo victim because Rachel had spent more than average time and energy, wisdom, and prayer to help Jenny's self-esteem and focus to be quite normal. She was far from promiscuous and was intimidated when it came to sex. She was terribly afraid of it.

Rachel had known since Jenny was small that she had a beautiful and passionate singing voice. She'd enrolled Jenny in voice lessons and piano. She helped her get involved with a modeling agency and Jenny was paid $10.00 per hour just to advertise products in the malls, even securing a live Barbie exhibit that paid a little more and had great exposure to be discovered by other agencies.

Paul was enamored by the modeling status and pursued her like there was no tomorrow. Jenny liked him as a friend and certainly enjoyed the attention but would tell Rachel after her dates with Paul that she wanted only to be friends and was uncomfortable about his romantic interest in her. After dating several weeks, she had planned to tell him.

The night she'd planned to tell him, he must have sensed the lack of connection he desired and asked Jenny what her deepest, darkest secret was. Jenny told him she was not comfortable talking about it. He then told her his deepest, darkest secret. He said that he'd been raped at the age of sixteen by a manager where he had worked in the mall. He claimed that after closing one night, the manager held a gun to his head and raped him. Jennifer cried, held him, was shocked at how he must have felt and allowed her heart to welcome him as more than a friend. She ended up telling him that night what <u>her</u> dark secret was.

A couple of days later, Paul wanted to tell Rachel what had happened to him and in tears declared his story. Rachel was distraught, asked if he'd told anyone else and he vigorously shook his head while holding Jenny around the waist burying his head in her chest as if he could not bear this memory alone clinging to her as if she were his life support and goal for every future hope. Rachel compassionately suggested that it would be best if he told his parents. He would not consider it.

Rachel was concerned about the future problems these

two would have if they indeed stayed together and ended up extremely close. Her fears were realized when after they dated steady for several months, they made their desire known to marry. Heath and Rachel talked with them at length about the necessity of Jenny's finishing school. Their need for time and counseling. Rachel was concerned that married life could possibly upset her school involvement and Heath promised to not allow that to happen. Still Rachel would not give her support to the marriage. It was months of dates and visits, and their closeness grew to a capacity that could not be understood. They confronted Heath and Rachel on their desire for a wedding and said that they would elope without their consent. They told his parents the same thing and both sets of parents got together over dinner one night to discuss the problem. His parents, still in the dark about Paul's sexual assault, felt that Jenny was the one for him. But they were apprehensive about the marriage taking place so soon, as was Heath. Rachel felt an inside connection with both of them and seemed to be the only one on Paul and Jenny's side wanting more than anything for her daughter to be happy, loved and healed as Heath's love had helped so much to heal her.

Rachel had known Jenny's eating disorder was beginning to change from bulimia to anorexia and had been concerned. But when Jenny admitted to bingeing and vomiting, Rachel was more than concerned. She began talking to counselors about what to do and contacted some of the best clinics specializing in eating disorders and the link from sexual abuse. Everyone was so helpful, supportive, convinced that their institution had the highest success rate and wanted to get this child well. Except when they found out Rachel couldn't produce $72,000.00 up front to secure a bed in the facilities. Some were willing to take half up front and the other half upon completion of a 10 week to 14-week inpatient program. Insurance wouldn't cover this type of treatment and though they could have gotten her on a scholarship program for less money, it was still more of a substantial amount than Heath and Rachel could raise.

When the suggestion of going away to a free ministerial program in Tennessee that Jenny would have to be accepted into for a minimum of 6 months, she flatly refused, and Paul supported her decision promising to help her with the eating disorder. All applicants had to sign a contract of agreement and willingness of cooperation to be accepted. That was the end of that, and Jenny promised not to endanger her health by bingeing and purging. Rachel had no choice but to trust her and pray.

After much discussion and Jenny's threat to leave with Paul, desiring her parents blessing but willing to proceed without it, Rachel began to plan the wedding. She got input from Jenny and Paul trying to accumulate enough information to make it special for them and beautiful. Which it was. Jenny's gown fit her 5'9", size 6 frame like a dream of perfection. It was a low, scalloped lace cut neckline with lace cap sleeves off the shoulders fitting close to just past her slim waistline V-Ing the front and back with a beautiful V in the back almost to the waist over a Cinderella, antebellum skirting. The hem line was scalloped in the same lace with a four-and-a-half-foot train gracing a satin bow at the catch up clips in back for the reception. The veil she chose was a simple pearl embellished band with three and a half feet of double layered tulle that she wore over her thick beautifully free flowing sable hair styled with minimum fuss left to curl slightly under just above her creamy mocha tanned shoulders. She wore white satin slippers and a simple droplet diamond earring and necklace set that set off the dress and her eyes like sparkling splendor. Her bouquet was white roses and beautiful periwinkle blue delphiniums. The maid of honor and bridesmaid's dresses were the color of Paul's eyes, sky blue. The wedding was phenomenally beautiful, and Paul cried when giving his vows. The reception was conducted by a wonderful disc jockey playing all their favorite love songs. During the first dance with Bride and Groom, a bubble machine filled the dance floor and continued through the Father and Daughter dance. There wasn't a dry eye in the place. Everyone there commented on how obviously in love they were, and they made an exquisitely beautiful couple with Paul several inches taller than Jenny and their hair identical in color.

It took about two months for trouble to start and by the third month, Paul had confessed that he had lied about the rape at gun point, and when he took his vows, he confessed that he was lying. He said that he had never loved her, and that he wanted out of the marriage. He confessed that he knew he was losing her the night he made up the lie. He could not cope with losing her at that time, knowing the lie would keep her close to him.

Jenny came home to Heath and Rachel in pieces, laying her head in Rachel's lap and asking if she could come home. She wouldn't eat for days, and Rachel could hardly get her to respond to her at all. She was so thin already, Rachel feared she might lose her. Jenny slept in the bed with Rachel and would cry herself to sleep every night while Rachel held her as if she were still four years old. After a few months Heath and Rachel helped Jenny get the marriage annulled declaring the marriage had been based on fraudulent behavior by Paul. It took more than a year for Jenny to recover from the failed marriage. It's hard to know if she ever did. She had an exceedingly difficult time with male relationships afterwards.

CHAPTER 16
THE ANGEL

It had been early in the year 2000 when Jackson and Mara had had the major disturbance which questioned the safety of the children and the possibility of their ending up in Jackson's custody. Rachel became more involved than ever trying to get Mara to agree to give Stephen to her. Mara refused on every hand and Rachel fell into a depression. But rather than sit around in despair, she began an all-out war campaign against the evil that seemed to be trying to snuff out Stephen's precious little light. But she would kindle it at every turn and every chance she got to speak with Stephen, she sang to him about Jesus, she prayed with him for angels to protect him when he relayed nightmares to Rachel. He would beg Rachel to come to his house and Rachel would usually cry half the night after he'd done it. She prayed for guidance and stayed close, remarkably close to what she perceived the will of God to be. She prayed for insight, peace, protection and mercy for Mara and her entire family. Blessings on the newest members which now numbered two. Little Jack was born August 8, 1999, and Rachel was beginning to feel overwhelmed, but she tried to connect with the entire family on a higher level of good than on a personal level of rescuing Stephen.

In July, Rachel planned another trip to Alaska to celebrate the birthdays of all three of her grandchildren being careful not to single out Stephen for special treatment fearing it would cause even further family discord.

She packed her nice summer clothes expecting warm weather and wore a cool, white cotton blouse with gray rayon casual dress pants and slip-on black sandals. It was a wonderfully pleasant trip and she stayed in close communication with her Heavenly Father knowing that He was the only key capable of unlocking the doors that would lead Stephen to the safety of Rachel's care.

The closer she got to Alaska, the lower the temperature dropped and at the Seattle plane change she thought hard about buying one of those stupid tourist sweatshirts until she noticed the price tag at $39.50. They had to be kidding, she'd freeze first she told herself and almost did when the plane she'd boarded flew into Anchorage air space. It was 21 degrees and the terminal leading to the airport felt even colder but Mara stood anxiously waiting in shorts and a tee shirt.

Rachel tried to concentrate on seeing the children rather than the temperature and soon was in the back seat of Mara and Jackson's Ford Explorer getting her first glimpse at Little Jack, Monica, and Stephen, wild with excitement in the midst of Rachel's hungry hugs. The silence captured Rachel and Mara, but the tears flowed freely with joy and conflicting emotions for them both as they made the drive to Mara's trailer. Neither Little Jack nor Monica was too keen on Rachel and didn't think they wanted to make friends, so she allowed Stephen all the attention he wanted until Monica, feeling left out, tried her hand at cuddling and playing seeming jealous of Rachel receiving Stephen's affection, attention, and undeniable love.

It was an enchanted visit and excitement seemed to run like electricity through the thread of family love, acceptance, and mystery in Rachel's heart until the new wore off of Jackson and Rachel's strained relationship. He seemed quite uncomfortable after only a few days and began to stay gone a good bit, coming back high on cocaine. Jackson seemed very much to want to entertain Rachel; this visit even more so than previous visits and Rachel tried to be appreciative though it was always a strain on her nerves because of the way they always seemed to ignore the children unless they caused a major disturbance. Rachel surmised it was to make up for his past undeniably injurious behavior earlier in the year when he came close to getting things done in such a manner as to possibly get custody of Monica and Little Jack enabling him to keep them from leaving Alaska. Knowing Mara would never leave her children behind he had her completely. He forced her to marry him that year and while taking video recordings of scenery shots, made a point of taping the marriage license. Rachel knew then that Mara was indeed in a mess Rachel could not get her out of this time. Not without God. There was nothing impossible for Him. She had had to put things totally in His hands after consulting every possible authority on Mara's rights and learning about Alaska law being vastly different from Alabama law. Children born in Alaska are considered

Alaskan citizens and, therefore, protected under Alaskan law to remain there against insurmountable odds. It seemed Rachel and Jackson now had a healthy fear of each other. Jackson feared Rachel might find a way of sneaking Mara out of Alaska and the kids out with her and Rachel feared Jackson's legal hold on Stephen because of his mental hold on Mara. It was an intensity that laid just under the surface of Rachel and Jackson's tolerant relationship with Mara and Stephen being the only cohesion between them.

Jackson tried to find things and scenes to impress Rachel and took everyone out to one of his favorite restaurants. It was a large and nice one with the huge, mounted head of a buffalo above the entrance door. While waiting to be seated, the children gravitated to the large glass case just inside the foyer area which held a huge brown bear inside, stuffed by an obviously talented taxidermist. The eyes appeared to be looking right at you when you chanced to look at them and his massive, clawed feet were positioned on large stones surrounded by foliage and branches appearing to be in his natural habitat.

When they were seated and had ordered, there seemed to be a strange tension between Jackson and Mara over a supposed look by Jackson at an attractive woman several tables away. When the food arrived and their appetites were almost appeased, the argument began to get heated and turned into an embarrassing disturbance at which point Rachel became disgusted with their insensitively rude manner and quietly reprimanded them both. She pushed her chair back as if to leave insisting that she couldn't believe their behavior. Mara quickly apologized promising to stop their display and Rachel stayed observing how quickly they were able to both ignite and extinguish their heated debates.

Stephen and Monica both wanted Rachel's lap and she noticed how rough Monica was when positioning herself for close seating. Rachel's heart broke a little more realizing how rough they must be with her for her to have such a rough manner, digging elbows and inconsiderately bouncing, shifting, and loudly requesting whatever it was she felt she would be cheated out of if she were not extremely assertive.

Later that evening they all sat around and watched T.V. a bit. Jackson seemed edgy and finally left the room leaving it to Rachel, Stephen, and Monica, since Mara was separating laundry. Monica had been sitting in Rachel's lap until, being short attention spanned, she'd gone to her room to play with her toys. As soon as she'd left, Stephen had taken her spot having been reprimanded earlier by Jackson for not letting Monica have equal time. When Monica returned and saw Stephen in her previous place of honor in Rachel's lap, she punched him in the chest as if she were doing nothing more than scratching an itch. She then walked past them both and Stephen stuck his foot out at just the right time to trip her at which time a fight like Rachel had never seen took place. They tumbled onto the floor like a ball, pulling each other's hair with one hand and punching each other with the other. Rachel broke up the fight and tried to explain why we just don't do that. Rachel was mortified at the primitive behavior these babies engaged in and it was obvious they were alone quite a bit.

The following day was the birthday party and in the little two-bedroom trailer where Little Jack slept in a playpen in the crowded living room or with his Mom and

Dad, Rachel planned the shopping trip for all the party things they would need. Stephen's birthday was late July, Monica's late October and Little Jack's was mid-August. They had planned to combine them knowing it wouldn't seem fair to come for Stephen's birthday and not the others. She first remembered she hadn't prayed and read her Bible, so she sat on Monica's bed where she had slept with Stephen and Monica. She found a place and had begun to read when Stephen came in.

"What cha' doin,' Granny?" Stephen asked looking at the Bible as if he'd never seen one before.

"I'm reading the Bible!" Rachel answered and at his confused look she added, "It's a book that tells us all about God."

The amazement was evident on his sweet little face as he asked in stunned revelation, "A book about God?" and he began searching through the Bible, turning pages as if he might see a picture of Him.

"Yes," Rachel answered evenly. "It tells us about how God sent his Son to us a long time ago to help us on Earth so we would never be alone. Even when we're scared or angry and we think we're bad because we're angry, He always loves us, and He doesn't think we're bad.

His silence was his acknowledgment that he understood more than Rachel could have known because Stephen had obviously been depending on God in his own way for a long time in his short little life.

"After I get finished reading, we're going to get ready for the party when we get back from the store!," Rachel told him excitedly and went back to reading. Several moments passed in silence and when Monica called for him, he ran out to see what she wanted.

When Stephen left the room, Rachel prayed, "Oh! Father, see how badly these children need You! They need to be taught about You, God. They need to grow up in the peace and safety of Your love. Please give them to me so that I can teach them about You, Lord."

Rachel then saw a vision of Stephen and Monica that appeared to the eyes of her troubled heart. She saw the children as a silhouette of gray, standing together as if they were blank pages needing the life of God's Word to be complete and Rachel cried, "See, God, they are so empty, so in need of someone to teach them about You and Your ways!"

Rachel felt a calm peace and heard the Spirit of God say to her spirit, as he allowed her to see another silhouette appearing to be Jackson and Mara, "You see them (the children) like that. I see them (Jackson and Mara) like that".

Rachel now understood that God Himself was protecting this family even though it appeared to Rachel that they were in the bowels of desecrating sin and danger. The sin being Jackson's cocaine habit and the danger being their work together for the Drug Enforcement Alliance (DEA). Evidently, Jackson had been in enough trouble with drugs previously that his freedom now depended on his success at undercover infiltration of the large suppliers and Mara was employed as well due to her close affiliation with him. Rachel's faith, however, had now been restored. She had heard from God and felt His insurmountable peace in the midst of this dangerous life her little girl had allowed her family to become so involved in.

After the party which was a huge success with all the children and Mara's tearful capturing of it all on film,

(Jackson had left earlier, giving no reason, which was not unusual) Rachel and Mara were finally alone to talk.

Rachel questioned her on her feeling of necessity to stay in a marriage that was obviously dysfunctional to the point of danger for her, psychologically and possibly even physically, observing his temper. Mara began to look paranoid and asked Rachel not to talk like that. Rachel tearfully hugged her and whispered how special she was to her, how much she missed her, how much she missed watching her grandchildren grow up knowing her and loving her.

Mara put her finger over her mouth and looked suspiciously out the door pulling away from Rachel's embrace. She looked out the windows, out into the yard as if they were under surveillance. She then turned on the stereo and asked Rachel if she'd like to sit out on the front deck and see the flowers, she'd picked several days ago. She was speaking inconsequentially, all the while cutting her eyes at Rachel and putting her finger up to her mouth as if to shush her.

"Sure," Rachel answered and followed her to the small wooden deck that was attached to the front of the trailer gracing a spacious yard of small trees and wildflowers colored vivid blue, yellow and fuchsia, orange that bordered one edge of the wildly growing, lush green grass.

After Mara had made a visual scope of the entire area appearing to nonchalantly survey the flowers, she sat next to Rachel on the stoop of the deck and began by tearing up in those beautiful almond shaped forest green eyes looking intently into Rachel's eyes as if crawling into her soul. She said, "Mama, we're in trouble and I'm fairly sure the trailer is bugged. I'm not sure who's had it done. The DEA or Mac, the leader of Alaska's biggest Hell's Angels' gang, and one of the biggest drug dealers in Anchorage."

Rachel tried not to show emotion but had known they were in danger somehow in the way a mother just knows. "Mara, please, let me help you get out of here. Please, Mara. Do you realize the danger these children are in?"

"Oh, it's not the children who are in danger, Mama. It's me and Jackson. My friends at the DEA are watching out for us. Really, don't worry about them. It may just be Jackson trying to keep me from sneaking out of Alaska with the children. I'm not sure who's doing it yet. I found a very sophisticated bug in the truck and when I told Jackson, he acted angry, but I couldn't read him well enough to know if he was angry at me or at not knowing who placed the bug there," Mara explained, as if this should clear up every fear Rachel had.

"Then let me take Stephen."

"I can't, Mama. He won't let me. He knows that I could get away a lot easier with one less child. I'm trapped, Mama," and the tears flowed in earnest.

Where are you, God? Rachel silently prayed, searching every minute area of her brain for a way to help her this time and a peaceful thought came through her soul. *This is not without God's knowledge nor is it too big for Him to fix.* She fell silent and gently laid her hand on Mara's that rested on her leg. "Mara, you don't forget who your Father is. Do you hear me, Baby?"

"I know, Mama. Believe me, we've been talking."

Later in the evening when Jackson and Mara were in their bedroom at the other end of the trailer and the smaller children were asleep, Rachel sat down in the living room by Stephen. He scooted over to give Rachel room and ended up on the arm of the recliner with his arm around Rachel's neck and his leg on Rachel's lap. The television was on cartoons and Rachel watched quietly with him for a while. A commercial came on and Rachel noticed he was staring at the window covering behind the television with a pensive look and a slight furrow to his little brow.

"What cha' thinkin' about, Baby?," Rachel asked.

"God," he answered softly never changing his gaze.

"He takes care of us, duttin' He," Rachel said as she lightly rubbed his little arm, so muscular to be so small.

"Unh huh," he said barely nodding his head.

"Stephen?" Rachel called quietly, "Do you have God in your heart?"

"Yep," he answered without hesitation and Rachel knew that he believed he did in such a way that that belief meant his survival. He held onto that for life.

Rachel's eyes grew moist as she held his little body close. This little child that was so much a part of her heart and soul. So very much.

Later that night Rachel and Mara had a semiprivate heated debate that turned almost ugly when Rachel tried once again to take Stephen. "Just a visit," she begged.

"No, Mother!" she'd cried desperately as if she were afraid for her life if Rachel persisted. Finally, Rachel dropped the issue.

The following day, Rachel's flight out of Anchorage was set for 11:00 a.m. It had been a good visit, overall. They'd gone to the zoo, to Portage Glacier, had eaten Halibut at a small restaurant hidden from the hustle and bustle of Anchorage some fifty miles away in a small town called Whittier. They'd gotten there by driving through a five-mile tunnel dug through the middle of one of the largest mountains in Alaska. The sights were wonderful. They'd seen a whale, but Rachel had seen far more than she cared to concerning the manner in which Jackson treated Stephen. It was nothing you could put your finger on other than contempt for his presence. *But then why did he want to keep him there. Leverage with Mara? Money from the Alaska yearly dividends that paid $1500.00 per child. Or control of Rachel's heart, knowing her love for Stephen.* Rachel couldn't figure it out and was forced to trust her Father in Heaven to know the best avenues for them all.

Rachel was awakened the next morning by Monica's squeals as she played a cat and mouse game with Stephen on the bunks where Rachel slept on the bottom, double size bunk. She smiled at their play and stretched dreading the leaving of these babies in this unstable environment they were born into. The fear tried to clutch Rachel's heart in an unbreakable vise, but she held onto faith that her Father would protect them and in time she knew that everything would work out for the best. He was Mara's Father, too. Rachel held on to that fact and the knowing that He was Stephen's protector, Monica's protector, Little Jack's protector. Rachel knew that where sin abounds, grace does much more abound, and she held on tight to the strength of that Word. She knew there were more angels on their side than there were evil influences on the other side.

The air was drenched with an ethereal tension as Rachel packed and made one last sweep of the trailer making sure she'd gotten everything. Stephen followed her around as if keeping her in his sight would prevent her from leaving. Rachel's heart was physically aching for him, knowing he wanted her to stay, knowing he wanted to be with her wherever she was, and it didn't matter where.

Mara tried to talk to him and explain that Granny had to go home, but he would not respond to what she said. Nor did he seem to compute it when Rachel explained the same thing. Rachel couldn't know what was going on in his little heart. The denial of reality he was emotionally forced into by his survival instinct. He was only five. What could he do but hope?

Soon they were at the airport and Rachel loved them all good and said good-byes. Stephen wouldn't tell her good-bye, he just continued drawing with his Etch-A-Sketch. She hugged him and kissed him, told him to be a good boy for his Mama and Daddy, that she would call him, and they could talk on the telephone, that he was going to school soon and wouldn't that be fun. Then she told him good-bye puzzled at his lack of emotion, his lack of response, he wouldn't even return the hugs and kisses.

"Come on, Mama. You'll miss your flight," Mara called as she unloaded Rachel's luggage from the back of the Explorer.

"Okay, I'm coming," she answered and kissed the babies one more time telling them she loved them and would see them soon, ending by cupping Stephen's little face for a final caress that would have to last until she didn't know when, swallowing the tears that threatened to tear her mind apart. "Bye, Baby, I love you," and she stepped away to rush to the Sky Cap and give Mara one last hug.

"I love you, Mama," Rachel said in a controlled croaking voice trying not to cry.

"Oh, Mara, I love you, please be careful and call me if you need me. I promise we can get you to safety," Rachel whispered in her ear so soft knowing she's still so young and afraid. She could feel it in her embrace.

"I'll be okay, Mama. I promise," she said with that

bulletproof persona that all 22-year old's have and Mara let her go walking backward and waving.

Rachel had gotten almost to the check in line when she heard Mara blow the horn of her car. It stopped Rachel in her tracks, and she dropped her luggage, turning to wave but Mara was pulled up closer to the front door and was waving Rachel back. Puzzled she went out to see what she wanted.

"Stephen wants to tell you bye, Mama. He thought if he didn't tell you bye that you wouldn't leave."

The avalanche of tears held back by sheer will power threatened to break through but only a few squeezed out as she ran to the open door where Stephen sat with his little round eyes filled with fear.

"Bye, Granny," he squeaked out as Rachel plunged into his little arms held out to her and she hugged him so close he'd have no doubt about her mutual dread of leaving.

"Bye, My Brave Little Warrior," she said as she kissed his quivering lip and cupped his little face not wanting to ever stop. "I love you so much, Baby. It's gonna be all right, I promise," and with that she turned before he could see the tears that would no longer obey her command to stay back.

She ran over to the Sky Cap to wave good-bye and the picture of his face as she left would haunt her forever. He couldn't wave at first. His eyes were red masked as a raccoon, he put up his little hand and Rachel put up hers until they drove out of sight, and she felt his misery like a ripping tear in her heart.

As Rachel sat in the airport waiting for the flight to be called, she opened her journal and let her pen be the connector of hope to faith to them that she had to leave in God's care for there was no other way.

I'm leaving Alaska and them to You, God
Remember they must have Your care
Remember their hope hidden deep in their hearts
Remember they need You right there.
I trust You, I must for my sanity's sake
You know that I do, or I couldn't go home
Remember, without them my heart will break
Please never leave them alone.
He seemed to reply in a soothing response calling me to come sit by His side.
Don't ever forget Little One Who I Am
I created all things and I know
The heart of love inside your soul
Just believe and great things I will show.

THE TRIP HOME WAS UNEVENTFUL, Rachel tried to see the beauty which passed beneath her and the jet. She saw wonders of mountains, great lakes, and great sights, but her heart remained fixed on His greatness in it all. The ability to bring peace to her weary mind about what could be in the hearts of those babies in the midst of constant danger, anger, selfishness, drugs, and poverty.

The following months were filled with phone calls and Rachel listened as Mara seemed to be hearing the voice of Wisdom, finally. There was also the voice of fear, and she didn't allow Stephen to talk to Rachel as much as Rachel would've liked. She'd enrolled him in school, they'd moved to a nice neighborhood, relatively speaking and he liked his teacher. A week had passed before the teacher wanted a conference with Stephen's mother. She'd conveyed that he might not be ready for school and that he didn't seem to be able to concentrate.

"Who is Jackson?," Stephen's teacher had asked Mara during the conference.

"That's Stephen's stepfather," Mara answered evenly.

"Stephen doesn't like him at all," the teacher conveyed.

Mara didn't know what to say and the teacher continued. "I need to have a conference with Jackson as soon as possible. Could you arrange that?", she asked pointedly.

"Sure," Mara answered feeling a bit nervous.

The conference was scheduled for the following day and Jackson would've done anything to get rid of Stephen every day, so he consented and met with the teacher.

She began with polite introductions and got down to business. "Did you know that Stephen has a substantial problem with the relationship you two have with each other?"

Jackson began to cast blame on Stephen's incapacity to listen and his rebellion against authority causing the teacher concern for Stephen's ability to flourish in his care. She gave him a serious talk about how important it was for Jackson to bond with Stephen and then said, "You don't want to be responsible for this child ending up being a problem in society. It is imperative that you bond with this child. Do you understand where I'm going with this?," she asked.

The following day Mara called Rachel and voiced her concern, finally, for Stephen's inability to grow up emotionally healthy in their care. She revealed her fears about

Stephen growing up to be a school shooter and told Rachel all about the teacher conference.

Rachel listened quietly knowing that God had indeed protected Stephen and was one step away from giving him to her for good, but Rachel said nothing of this. She just listened.

When Mara reached the end of her fearful speech, she began to cry asking Rachel what she was going to do. Rachel thought for a moment and said, "What do you want to do?"

"I don't know what to do, Mama. Jackson's never been able to deal with him," she said, and Rachel could almost see Mara's troubled face covered with guilt and shame at her inability to raise him as she'd hoped. It hadn't turned out a bit like she'd wanted, and she loved her little boy more than she ever knew she could. Enough to let him go to the safe environment of her mama's house, where he would flourish and grow up loved, accepted, properly disciplined with every advantage that she'd had and realized now, hadn't taken advantage of.

"Now, you know, Mara, that I'll have to have temporary custody in writing to get him enrolled in school and all his records, certificates, social security card. All that," Rachel said firmly, surprised at her own strength, faith and maturity.

"I know, Mama, we'll do all that and Jackson will buy the plane tickets. When do you think you can come?" she asked, seeming anxious.

"Well, let me talk to Daddy and see what he thinks, and I'll call you back," Rachel said.

"Tonight?" Mara asked.

"I'll try, Honey. Don't worry. Daddy has wanted him out

of Jackson's influence for a while.," she said gently. "I'll call you back."

"Okay. Bye, Mama, I love you," she said sounding more defeated than Rachel ever remembered her sounding, but determined to do the right thing

"Bye, Baby," and she hung up thanking God for answering her prayers.

After speaking with Heath, they both agreed that they should move quickly before Mara changed her mind or Jackson moved them again making it impossible to find them. So, Rachel made the call to Mara to finalize their plan.

"Have you asked Stephen if he wants to do this, Baby?," Rachel asked knowing the answer.

"Oh yes, Mama. Are you kidding? You know he does."

"Are you okay with it, Mara?" Rachel asked.

"Yeah, I'm okay. I'll miss him but I know it's the best thing," she said sadly. "Of course, Jackson doesn't think we should cater to his whims. He thinks with me though that he'd be better off with you."

Heath drove Rachel to the Hartselle Airport in Atlanta to catch her flight on a cold, slushy day in late November 2000. She tried to keep her mind from thinking something would go bad wrong and they'd change their minds when she got there or something else even worse, she wouldn't even let her mind entertain.

Rachel's adrenaline pumped through her body in what seemed like mass production, and she couldn't stop smiling as she kissed Heath good-bye and thanked him again for loving her and her babies. The light shone from his eyes like sapphires, and he smiled that shy little smile that had been lighting up her world since the first time she'd seen him.

"I love you, "she whispered in his ear lightly touching it

with her lips and hugged him one more time just a little too tight.

"I love you, too, Rachel," he breathed. "Be careful," he said, as he grabbed her luggage and walked toward the door to the terminal handing it to her with a look of total admiration for her desire to raise this troubled little boy when he knew she was tired beyond words.

"I will!," she called back over her shoulder disappearing down the boarding plank leading to the Boeing that would take her to her babies and in particular the one she knew she was destined to raise.

Heath watched from the huge windows by the terminal and waited until the plane lifted off the runway before returning to his car, praying for God to keep Rachel safe and bring her back home safe with Stephen.

After she found her seat on the plane and got her things situated, she sat down and got out her journal writing down emotions too great to express in the spoken word to anyone but God.

November 2, 2000

Thursday Entry

Back to Anchorage to see my little Sunshine. God, let Your light shine upon her forever. In my purse is a boarding pass for Stephen. It's hard to believe he'll be coming home with me. It's been so long since I've had real time with him. I wish I could take Monica, too. My heart has been knitted to them both.

God, give me the grace to continue to trust You with Stephen's life. Help me to remember that though I will have more physical influence, it will be Your spiritual influence that will heal him from the wounds of the past.

Oh, to hold him in my arms and fill his little world with the love I have for him. To look at him and hold his hand. To watch him sleep and hear him laugh again. To see him warm, safe, and whole.

Help me, Father, to remember to keep him in Your hands more than mine. In Your Name, Jesus...Amen

WHEN RACHEL ARRIVED at the airport in Anchorage, Mara met her alone. Rachel's heart sunk, wondering why she'd not brought the children to meet her, but she remained calm and hugged her baby. Mara explained on the way that they'd had to move and had been unable to find a place, so they were staying in a hotel.

Rachel was shocked when she saw the room. It was decorated in 1970's green and looked like it could've been that old. The room had two queen sized beds one of which Jackson laid up on watching television. The babies were dirty and there was dirty laundry piled up in the entrance to the bathroom. The room had a kitchenette that was piled high with dirty dishes and the table wasn't wiped off from the last meal which could only be described as a chaotic situation meal of smearing the food on it lavishly by the children.

Mara apologized for the mess and said she didn't have time to clean as she helped Rachel place her bags next to the bed that was made perfectly knowing Mara had made a clean bed priority for her mother.

Stephen was beyond excited and began to show a little attitude toward Monica right away as he jumped from his bed and ran into Rachel's arms. Rachel had to hold a tight rein on her emotions and her extreme desire to tell Jackson what she thought of him. She felt sure Stephen felt the same way.

She gave Monica equal attention and when she sensed Jackson's last attempt to put Stephen in his place, she was careful to try not to interfere knowing Jackson would love the opportunity to kill Rachel's hope and make Stephen stay just to prove his control. Rachel felt as if he had her by the throat and could tighten the noose at any time. Rachel had explained that they had to stay just a few more days when it became obvious Stephen was ready to go right then. At his confused look of what a day was, she explained it in sleeps on her fingers. Every night for three days at bedtime we counted down the sleeps.

After watching the family in action over the next few days it broke Rachel's heart to see how the younger children were allowed to take advantage of everything Stephen had, including his food. His only defense was to eat as fast as possible before they climbed up on the table and literally grabbed the food from his plate. Monica and Little Jack looked well fed and plump, where Stephen was very thin, and his belly protruded reminding Rachel of the starving Ethiopian children she'd seen on T.V.

Jackson was quite irritable the entire time Rachel was there, and she prayed for the time to pass quickly knowing that she would lose it if Jackson attempted to lay a hand on Stephen now. Rachel tried to keep the mood light and keep the children entertained and out of Jackson's way while she was there.

Finally, it was time for good-byes and Rachel empathized with Mara knowing how hard it must have been to know she was all but giving away her firstborn son and would miss him beyond words, beyond all reason, beyond anything she'd ever experienced in her battered life. This would hurt the most, eventually.

Rachel told her how proud she was of Mara for making this decision. How well she would take care of Stephen. How she would always tell him how much his mother loved him by doing this. After hugs, kisses and Mara leaving as soon as possible warning Rachel not to cry or she would cry too and not be able to stop, Mara hugged her son for the last time and drove away with Monica crying for Stephen.

CHAPTER 17

THE BEGINNING OF THE HEALING

It was sheer relief to get checked in at the airport and move close to the terminal. Rachel bought Stephen what he wanted for breakfast while they awaited their flight to be called. She had to tell him several times that it was all his and to slow down. He'd gotten in the habit of eating so fast, it came right back up when he finished the entire sausage biscuit, and he ran to the garbage to expel it there.

Rachel fought back the anger that tried to overtake her, concerning Jackson's disregard for Stephen's need for the simplest of things, like food. She told him it was fine, and she soothed him with the maternal instinct that had been a natural thing since the day he was born. She bought him some juice and snacks for the plane ride and prayed for healing for him.

In the weeks and months that followed, Rachel found out many disturbing secrets. One of the most disturbing was the fact that Jackson had kicked Stephen in the chest one time hard enough to knock the wind out of him. "And, and I couldn't breathe, Granny.," he had said with wide eyes as he played with his tub toys floating in his bath water one peaceful bath time evening.

Rachel told Mara at the first available time, but Mara questioned Jackson and after his denial, found it hard to believe. Rachel had him checked out from head to toe immediately by Hannah's pediatrician. Stephen had many challenges to overcome in the next two years but with doctor's care, counseling, church activities, Heath, Rachel, Jenny, and Hannah's love, he began to blossom. He had one and a half years of kindergarten because when Rachel first got him, he didn't even know his basic colors. His little mind was like a sponge, and he absorbed everything he could mentally contain.

At this time, he has one season of coach pitch baseball behind him and can read several words. He is happy and wants to live with his Granny and Papa forever. He had heard his Papa answer the telephone: Heath Billings Roofing, so many times that when he expressed a desire to be named after his Papa, he insisted on learning the spelling of the complete name believing his last name would be Roofing. Hannah had prayed years ago for a little brother and now that prayer also has been answered. Heath had always wanted a son and now he has one. Stephen goes with him to work sometimes, and his Papa lets him get up on the roof, ride in the truck and play on the ladders. Stephen is happy. Mara on the other hand has had a challenging time.

In July 2001, she began missing Stephen so badly and her relationship had become so unbearable with Jackson that she began calling most every day. Some days they didn't have money to feed the children and Rachel would ask Heath if they could wire them enough to buy food. Mara would tell Rachel how bad things were and how they now lived in a little motor home in a neighbors' yard. That Jackson was so strung out on drugs that she would buy a lot of food at one time and that she missed Stephen more than she'd ever know she could miss anything or anyone.

Rachel decided it time for a strong, tough love talk, again. Only this time she didn't have to worry about Stephen getting caught in the blame game fallout and she let her have it.

Rachel tried to talk sense into her befuddled brain trying to wake her up to the reality of where her life was most definitely headed.

Their voices became somewhat raised and it appeared to any listener that they were fighting. Stephen, hearing the conflict, left his world of cartoons and stood at the door of Rachel's office asking why she was fussing with his Mama. Rachel explained that they weren't fussing, just disagreeing, which didn't seem to make a dent in his concerned little mind, and he came over and crawled up in Rachel's lap.

Now Rachel had known within the first three weeks she had him that he hated Jackson and feared him. Rachel remembered how obsessed he'd been about wanting to grow up fast and be a giant so he could beat Jackson up. This mode of thought had reached a point of major concern when the only way Rachel could get him to eat healthy food was telling him that he needed it to make his body strong and grow up big. He would eat anything when motivated that way and seemed to be unusually quiet at times seeming to daydream of the day when it would happen. It seemed to be his goal in life. That dazed expression he used to get was back on his face as he sat close to Rachel's chest looking up at her with fear in his eyes.

"What's wrong, Baby?" Rachel asked smoothing Stephen's hair and looking in his eyes.

"Why are you fussing at my Mama?," he asked as if she'd gone into his sacred toy box and bagged them up for disposal.

"We're not mad at each other, we're just trying to agree on something," Rachel explained gently.

"But when my Mommy fusses, my Daddy hits my Mommy," he said genuinely frightened that this may take place and Rachel's adrenaline froze in its tracks shutting down her heightened emotions.

Rachel smoothed his hair back again and kissed him on the cheek, whispering in his ear, "Granny won't fuss with Mommy anymore, Baby, I promise. Now don't worry. Okay?"

He didn't appear to be comforted sufficiently and Rachel felt he needed to talk about this but now was not the time though she had to know. "Honey, don't worry, now. Okay? Your Mommy's strong, she's not gonna let your Daddy hurt her. Does she ever hit him back?", she questioned.

"Yeah, Mommy tries, but he's too strong and Mommy can't never win," he said as he dropped his little head and looked at his hands lying upward in his lap.

Rachel was speechless and numb.

"Would you go get my Mommy?" he asked looking up and penetrating Rachel's soul with his round intense blue gaze.

Rachel was in shock and told Mara to just hang on a second while she tried to think of what to say to her brave little warrior who'd lived so much pain already in his short little five and a half years.

"Mommy's gonna be okay, Baby," Rachel soothed. "Your

Daddy and Mommy aren't fussing anymore. Everything's fine. Don't worry now. Okay? Go watch your cartoons and Granny will tell Mommy she's sorry for fussing. Okay?"

"Okay, Granny," he said slipping down from Rachel's lap and slowly walking back into the living room to catch up on Sponge Bob Square Pants knowing his only choice is to trust God with everything dear like his Granny had taught him.

"Mara!", Rachel questioned quietly with an urgency and demanding manner. "Did you hear what Stephen said?"

"Yeah, Mama. I heard," Mara answered with a deflated mien.

"Is it true, Mara? Does he hit you?" Rachel asked intently, trying to keep her voice down low so as not to let Stephen hear.

"Yeah, Mama," Mara said shamefully, "It's true."

"Oh, Mara," Rachel sighed, and the tears began to make trails on the receiver. "Please, Mara, please let me help you get out. Baby, please come home."

Mara was silent for several moments and Rachel wondered what she was thinking but not willing to break in on her private reality of resourceful decisions. Finally, Mara said in an incredulous little girl voice Rachel hadn't heard in many years, "Can I come home, Mama?"

"Yes, Baby," she sobbed. "Of course, you can come home."

The next several weeks were filled with secretive and careful planning as Rachel read maps, made calls to shelters bordering Anchorage. The only way to get out safely was to get a ride to a small town in Canada, stay overnight in a shelter and ride a bus to Seattle to catch a flight home. The catch was getting away from Jackson before he could alert the authorities at the border and stop her from leaving

Alaska if he found her missing because they would definitely detain them and refer them to the Magistrate on Jackson's report of kidnapping.

When the plans were finalized, Mara called and told Rachel she was ready, and that Jackson was asleep, so she'd rolled the car to a safe distance to crank it and was calling from the store five miles from the campground. Rachel instructed her to leave the car, get a cab to the Days Inn and call her when she got to the room.

"Room!" Mara gasped. "How am I going to get a room? I only have $30.00."

"I've already gotten you a room, Mara. Just go in and tell them you're Tamara March. They'll give you the key and walk you to your room, then call me."

"Okay, Mama," Mara's surprised response evident in her tone. "I love you, Mama," she said.

"Be careful, Mara and stay out of sight. If you need anything for the babies, order room service. I don't want you out of that room until you catch the 6:00 a.m. bus. And don't talk to anyone. Act like you're just out shopping. I love you, Baby."

Rachel and Heath decided it would be a good day to take the kids to the beach after Mara had all her instructions, flight times and numbers. She also had Heath's toll-free number to his cell phone, so they all went to the beach. They knew Jackson would be calling as soon as he found her missing and no one was comfortable enough to deal with him until Mara was way south in the "Lower 48". Rachel knew that once she touched Alabama soil, there would be nothing he could do.

Three days later Heath, Rachel and Stephen were waiting at the Hartselle Airport in Atlanta when Mara walked past the baggage claim holding Monica's little hand and Little Jack on her hip spotting her Mama and Daddy holding Stephen by the hand walking toward them.

Rachel ran to Mara and kissed her tear-streaked cheeks holding her face in both hands before hugging her and Little Jack together then picking Monica up excitedly and squealed, "Monica! It's Granny! Remember me?"

Her little eyes were wide with confused fatigue from the trip, but she laid her head on Rachel's shoulder hugging her with her chubby little arms saying in the sweetest little voice Rachel had ever heard, "Granny! I go to your house?"

"Yes, Baby, you're coming to Granny's house," Rachel answered as she leaned her head against Monica's soft blonde caramel colored hair.

They all got acquainted again, packed Mara's sparse belongings and went home. Stephen and Monica sat together in the back beside Little Jack's car seat Rachel had bought. Rachel took more pictures as Stephen and Monica would hug and talk. She'd gotten several at the airport when Mara tearfully hugged Heath, when Monica held her arms up for Heath to take her and when all three children hugged for the first time in well over a year.

Mara was happier to be home than Rachel remembered her being in a long time. They got loose ends tied up on Mara's residence and benefits for the children. Rachel bought Mara, Monica, and Little Jack several basic items of clothing and toiletries. Everyone got settled in a short span of time and evaded Jackson's constant calls by checking the caller ID but got quite a scare when the police showed up at Heath and Rachel's house saying they'd gotten a call from Alaska authorities warning that Mara, Monica, and Little Jack had been kidnapped and were being held by the Hell's

Angel's leader at Heath and Rachel address. They seemed to want to take them to the station immediately and extradite them to Anchorage, Alaska. Rachel and Mara's knees went weak, and they tried to explain the situation not seeming to be getting the message across adequately for the officer with his orders. Finally, Rachel sent Hannah inside to get Heath and after they talked several minutes, the officers seemed somewhat convinced but warned Mara not to leave town in case they needed to question her further. She assured them that she'd worked quite hard to get out of her dangerous situations in Alaska and had most definitely decided to stay with her mom.

Jackson didn't stop there and Mara, being spooked about what he might do next, called him, and told him where she was, why she had left and her plans to divorce him as soon as possible.

CHAPTER 18

THE CON, THE SYSTEM AND THE REPEATED VICTIMIZATION

Over the next several months, Jackson went through his gambit of tricks to get Mara back, but they all failed until he had an elaborate conversion experience to Christianity and wore her down until she believed that he really could've been changed by God. He wanted his family back, apologized to Stephen, drove to Alabama at significant risk considering he had a warrant in Alabama for his arrest and knowing he would face felony charges and incarceration. Within three to five months Jackson had Mara, Monica and Little Jack back in Alaska and had gotten Mara pregnant.

They were both arrested in early May 2002 for illegal sale of a vehicle. Jackson appeared to have accepted payment for an impounded car in his lot for the sum of $3,300.00 in cocaine after failing to adequately inform the owner of the sale.

Daniel, still in jail, but due for parole on May 6, 2002, happened to be the day Mara gave birth to her third son. Rachel received a phone call, two weeks before Daniel's parole hearing. It was from a parole officer, asking if she knew Daniel Mylar's sentence had been changed taking 50 years off his sentence; by a Montgomery County Circuit Court Judge making him very eligible for parole.

Rachel almost dropped the receiver but realized her body was frozen in the position and she could still hear the gentleman on the phone.

It seems that an error had been made in one of the judicial offices and none of the prosecuting officers had been notified either, and a hearing had been held to overturn the original judges' sentence which he had refused to do on five separate occasions due to the severity of the offense and Daniel's lack of cooperation. But the decision now stood, and Rachel would have to tell Mara and Jenny that Daniel might be released from prison.

Everything was going smoothly in Mara's life, temporarily, until Rachel told her she would need to deal with the rape issue again. It took Mara three and a half weeks to write a one-page letter stating that she had not fully realized the damage done to her by Daniel until she looked at their innocent, full of life and trust five-year-old daughter. She then realized that only an evil, sick and unmercifully selfish person could destroy beauty like that and that she was concerned for someone else's little girl suffering the endless fate of shame, fear, and guilt that she had experienced.

It was after the letter and the birth of her fourth child that their lives became so confusingly difficult. They claimed that the stress of dealing with Daniel's release was instrumental in their negligent paperwork and bad choices that set them up to be arrested on May 19, 2002.

Jackson's priors may sway the judicial system toward his

serving time in jail. Mara, with no priors and three small children in her care, may get five years' probation and a substantial fine.

Mara is now seeking a therapist to help her deal with her depression and stress.

When Jenny found out that Daniel's sentence had been changed and that his mother along with the rest of the family were still alleging that Rachel had made the whole rape, molestation story up to get back at Jackie for marrying Henry. And that they had somehow convinced even Henry's mother (who'd been very supportive of Rachel and her paternal grandchildren, Mara and Jenny up to this point) that Daniel deserved to have a life and be released from prison, Jenny became very angry and left immediately to "visit" her grandmother, requesting that Henry, her biological father, be there.

Rachel was frantically afraid that Jackie may hurt Jenny, knowing Jenny's temperamental tendencies. She begged Heath to stop her from going but even though she promised him she wouldn't, she went anyway.

Henry, not knowing the reason for her visit met her with enthusiasm but when all he wanted to talk about was old times, she reminded him that the hearing was coming up on May 6th.

"Do you even remember anything about all that, Jenny," he asked surprised, yet solemn.

Jenny looked him in the eyes and said with conviction, "I remember everything."

Henry didn't make it to the parole hearing but then neither could Jenny. Rachel had had to help her write a letter of protest but getting her to the hearing had been an impossibility because Jenny didn't want to face the memories that haunted her even in her sleep. She didn't feel she could without losing it, she had a fear of her own unknown.

Heath and Rachel were at the hearing, along with several victims' advocates, a representative from the Governor's Office and the District Attorney of Montgomery County.

On Daniel's side there were his mother, Jackie, Pastor Wendall Craig, Daniel's aunt and several distant family members. The Pastor spoke first and made Rachel sound like a manipulative, vindictive woman of questionable character who never shut up long enough for him to adequately assess the truth of Mara and Jenny's comments at the 1995 AG Office meeting. He further stated that Daniel had no hard feelings toward Rachel for making up this lie about him.

Jackie spoke next and spoke of her poor son growing up in prison and how she missed him. How Rachel had admitted to him that she'd planned to ruin his life to get back at his mother because Rachel didn't like her.

It was then Heath's turn and he spoke of the prison Mara and Jenny still lived in so much so that they couldn't even come to the hearings. How much emotional stress what Daniel had done to Rachel's daughters had caused her and how Rachel was even raising Mara's oldest son due to Mara's inability to do so.

Rachel spoke and showed pictures of the girls at the ages they were when Daniel had violated them. She told the Board of her lack of relationship, good or bad, with Jackie and her only problem being that she didn't adequately care for her girls while under Jackie's care. Rachel further stated her concern that Daniel may try to harm Mara and Jenny for telling on him, or her for supporting them and the problem she had with his refusal to confess what he had done asking for mercy as opposed to staying in denial which seemed extremely dangerous to Rachel

The Governor's representative spoke about the heinous crime Daniel was convicted of, describing in detail what he'd done and adamantly opposed his release requesting the Board to mandate that he serve all of his sentence.

The District Attorney spoke of Daniel's prison record and the numerous disciplinary offences along with his being caught with hollow point bullets, other weaponry contraband and drugs.

At the conclusion of the hearing and after a lengthy deliberation by the Board, the decision was to be continued until July 8th, 2002.

The DA and other supporters of the case were concerned that the Board had planned to parole Daniel but had possibly been unaware of his prison records showing the weapon contraband.

Many victims' advocates told Rachel that the feared Daniel would be paroled unless Mara or Jenny came to the next hearing.

Rachel's concern led her to speak with her and Jenny's medical doctor who'd been the director of the citywide child abuse center for several years before having her own practice.

Her concern was for Jenny's possible inability to cope with the pressure of telling what had happened to her at such an early age before so many strangers when Jenny had not adequately dealt with all the emotional issues she was trying to face at the present time. Rachel was in a quandary as to what to do so at the doctors' suggestion, she put the question to Jenny. After several attempts at trying to talk to Jenny about the next hearing, Jenny finally agreed.

Rachel told her that it was totally her decision whether to go or not and whether to speak or not.

Then she put the future possibility to Jenny by asking her what would be harder to manage, speaking at the hearing and Daniel likely staying in prison or running the risk of bumping into him at Walmart. Jenny responded with a comment Rachel refused to divulge to this author and had made her decision to attend and speak at the hearing within a matter of minutes.

During the time between May 6 and two weeks before the hearing Jenny became hysterical on more than one occasion and was arrested for minor possession of alcohol twice in the same weekend. The first time she was arrested, she was out with her friends and drank too much. One of her friends who happened to be male offered to take her home and she agreed walking with him to the door. When he took her arm to help steady her gait, she grew frantic and began to fight him yelling that he was trying to rape her.

Obviously upset, her friend asked her to sit on the curb and wait while he went in to get one of her close girlfriends. When he came out with her friend, he found that she'd gone to a fence and leaning back against it had her knees drawn up under her chin and was crying uncontrollably. Her girlfriend tried to talk to her, and she began sobbing and telling her that she'd been sodomized when she was young and that the man who did it had been in jail ever since, but he was going to get out soon and kill her family. Her friend tried to calm her, but Jenny got up and began to run down the street screaming someone was trying to rape her.

Jenny had no memory of her actions that night and had gone to jail for minor possession of alcohol. Her hysteria was so great and her manner so aggressive that the officers had to Mace her to keep her from hurting herself.

The second arrest was similar to the first except she was merely in her own vehicle and the same officer spotted it when they'd pulled off the road for Jenny to relieve herself and found her intoxicated again.

When Rachel bailed her out the next morning Jenny laid her head in Rachel's lap apologizing for the trouble she'd caused.

As July 8 grew closer Jenny grew more nervous but Rachel tried to calm her in every way, she could knowing it would be over soon if she could just get Jenny through the hearing.

On the day of the hearing Jenny began to feel sick after seeing her aunt at the hearing with one of Daniel's family members. One of the victim's advocates who was a close friend of Rachel's took her downstairs to get her something to eat and drink hoping it would settle her stomach. While they were downstairs the case was called and when Jenny came into the hearing room, she was accompanied by the Victim Service Officer for the Attorney General's Office on one side and Rachel's friend on the other. Of course, all eyes were on her, and she appeared quite reluctant. Rachel found out after the hearing that she'd told the VSO that she didn't think she was going to speak. The VSO said, "Fine, just go in and sit down by your mother." What Jenny didn't know was that Rachel was seated at the table where only those speaking at the hearing sit.

Henry DeVaughn was not there, and the Pastor was absent also, but Daniel's aunt spoke first. She said that Daniel begged her after his failed attempts at release to go to Rachel and beg her to tell the truth. She went on to say what a good boy he'd always been and humbly asked the Board to release him.

As Jenny listened to Daniel's support system bash Rachel's reputation and continue to defend Daniel's innocence, Rachel began to notice an indignant air begin to straighten Jenny's sitting position. She also noticed the dazed deer in the headlights look from when she'd first sat down being replaced with a poignant stare at the speakers. She then leaned over and whispered to Rachel, "I'm about to blow their crap away."

When Daniel's two spokespersons had had their say, the Board called Jenny up to speak. She got up and with dignity stood before the Board. What she said had not been written down. She didn't need notes to relay what had been imprinted on her little soul that had grown up with lightning speed at age three by Daniel's sick obsession with little girls. She'd lived it and when you see the devastating truth of what sexual abuse does to the adult struggling for life in the mind of the terrified three-year-old trapped there, it comes through just that way.

She began by saying, "My name is Jennifer Billings, and I don't really know what you want me to say. I know I was young when this happened to me, but I remember everything." She spoke less than three minutes but what she said was dynamite and when she could say no more without crying, never losing eye contact with the Board members, she sat down.

When Rachel looked at the Board's reaction to Jenny's statement, she saw the strongest inmate advocate wipe tears from her cheek in an attempt at regaining her composure. Of course, Rachel couldn't see clearly due to her own tears, but so admired Jenny's courage in coming forward with dignity and speaking of her private hell.

Rachel spoke next and told the Board how difficult it had been to get Jenny to the hearing. She told of the challenge it had been to keep Mara and Jenny alive due to the devastation of growing up in the aftermath of the crime done to them by Daniel. She closed with her concern and feeling of community responsibility to keep Daniel incarcerated as long as possible knowing the recidivism rate to be so high and hoping to save other little girls from this predator. She thanked the Board and sat down reaching over to clasp Jenny's quivering hand in hers. They both held on tight until the hearing was over.

The DA stood before the Board and concluded stating that everything she'd brought out in the previous hearing still stood. She refuted Daniel's good boy image by bringing up the hollow point bullets again and concluded her statement with her concern about Daniel's family being in denial with him and exhibiting the standard behavior of a perpetrator by blaming the victim.

The Board of Pardons and Paroles made their decision and announced Daniel's parole denied until 2005.

Collecting the feelings involved with sexual abuse is like trying to defuse an ignited bomb. The intensity of emotions loomed ever near like a cloud on a rainy day. You know the sun will shine again because God has promised never to flood the earth a second time with His rainbow, so the sexual abuse victim strives to wait out the rain but inwardly has a challenging time believing that the sun will ever shine for them again. With hope, love, and help, they continue to strive, distancing the abuse from them by going inside and watching scenes of sunny days on television or through relationships of helping others and trying to be the sun in someone else's life.

This is a poem written by Rachel in some of the darker days.

My Hero

I simply love the words You speak
That enter through my soul
Your blessings I hereby entreat
That I may be made whole
The hate within the world it seems
Brings sadness to my heart
It's only in the grace You bring
My heart's not torn apart
I set my heart on Your good love
Which brings me worlds of peace
Of riches and of promises
Of beauty and increase
Destroying evil things, we face
When searching out our goals
In filling up our deepest place
To liberate our souls...

EPILOGUE

When Rachel's private hell began, there was little effective help for victims of sexual abuse. There was much trial and error in finding help for the three of them. There are more now but much more support needs to be added. Education needs to be widespread about this misunderstood phenomenon of sexual abuse and how to prevent it.

There is a longing inside a broken soul that hungers for the nurturing love that should have been received as a child from the caretaker. There is a fast-running pace to keep one step ahead of the pain. In this race of life abuse survivors must run, they often collide with a person who has similar traits. This often attracts them to the familiar person and gets the mind confused with whom they looked to to meet their needs in childhood but to no avail. Their childlike desire and adult persona make them irresistible to their new collision. In their sub-conscience but formidable quest to recreate their past trauma yet this time feeling powerful enough to effect the outcome in a positive way, the world in store for them seems insurmountable along with their enormous confusion and stress. It was their child mentality that brought on the culmination of the relationship to begin with, and they have now become connected to the one thing in their past they wish they could forget. They are connected to the type of person who is not only incapable of meeting their needs but is attracted to the victimized mentality they unwittingly carry with them.

Though this entire scenario seems hopeless; it isn't. God in His sovereignty has created each of us with a God shaped void that no man can fill, only Him. Whether we were injured, neglected, abused, used, or tortured there is still a place within us all that only God Himself can satisfy. Not that we should not seek every educated hope for healing through the miracles man himself has the power to perform through unselfish love and faith. But ultimately, we will all have to come to the end of our own race from the pain into the race toward the arms of our Father who welcomes us and loves us and has already made every provision for us as is beautifully recorded in His Holy Word and the friendships of the brave survivors who choose to share their friendship with others who've been affected by the strange and challenging world we must learn to not only survive but thrive in, by helping others through sharing our lives with them.

Without the relationship Rachel holds very dear with Jesus Christ, due to her incredible story of abuse herself, she admits to a certainty of failure to survive.

About the Author

Judah Clarke has been writing poetry from an early age and felt it was her voice to God. She is a spiritual searcher and has felt God's purpose for her life a mystery until her empathic tendencies turned her toward injustice of the helpless. Mrs. Clarke has composed her poetry into poem books that she would give away to people she has met along her life journey. She has given copies of certain poems or personal poems she has written to bless and communicate with people.

Mrs. Clarke's work has been printed on beautiful formats and sold at craft shows. Some of her poetry hangs on walls of offices in various places. She was Poet Laureate of the Millennium of 2000 in an Anthology book and published in many others.

Mrs. Clarke has spoken on various occasions to groups about sexual abuse and has worked with law enforcement and crime victims' organizations. She has also worked personally with sexual abuse survivors for over twenty years. Judah has three grown children, several grandchildren, and great-grandchildren. She is married to a most wonderful man, lives in the South with him in their dream house in the country with their Great Pyrenees, The Queen.

They thank God every day for their wonderful life.

www.ingramcontent.com/pod-product-compliance
Lightning Source LLC
Chambersburg PA
CBHW072000290426
44109CB00018B/2084